IN THE WAKE

In

*

the

*

Wake

*

ON BLACKNESS AND BEING

CHRISTINA SHARPE

DUKE UNIVERSITY PRESS
Durham and London
2016

Designed by Amy Ruth Buchanan
Typeset in Arno Pro by
Tseng Information Systems, Inc.

Library of Congress Cataloging-in-Publication Data
Names: Sharpe, Christina Elizabeth, author.
Title: In the wake : on Blackness and being /
Christina Sharpe.
Description: Durham : Duke University Press, 2016. |
Includes bibliographical references and index.
Identifiers: LCCN 2016024750 (print) |
LCCN 2016025624 (ebook) |
ISBN 9780822362838 (hardcover) |
ISBN 9780822362944 (pbk.) |
ISBN 9780822373452 (e-book)
Subjects: LCSH: African Americans — Social conditions. |
Racism — Health aspects — United States. | Premature
death — Social aspects — United States. Discrimination in
law enforcement — United States. | Slavery — United
States — Psychological aspects.
Classification: LCC E185.625 .S53 2016 (print) |
LCC E185.625 (ebook) | DDC 305.896/073 — dc23
LC record available at https://lccn.loc.gov/2016024750

Cover art: Cornelia Parker, *Hanging Fire (Suspected Arson)*, 1999. Charcoal, wire, pins, and nails; 144 × 60 × 72 inches. The Institute of Contemporary Art/Boston, Gift of Barbara Lee, The Barbara Lee Collection of Art by Women, 2006.5. Courtesy of the artist and Frith Street Gallery, London. Photo by Jasmine Fu.

FOR THOSE WHO HAVE DIED RECENTLY.

IdaMarie Sharpe

Caleb Williams

Stephen Wheatley Sharpe

*

FOR THOSE WHO DIED IN THE PAST

THAT IS NOT YET PAST.

Van Buren Sharpe Jr.

Robert Sharpe Jr.

Jason Phillip Sharpe

Van Buren Sharpe III

*

FOR THOSE WHO REMAIN.

Karen Sharpe

Annette Sharpe Williams

Christopher David Sharpe

Dianna McFadden

*

FOR ALL BLACK PEOPLE WHO, STILL,

INSIST LIFE AND BEING INTO THE WAKE.

*

FOR MY MOTHER

Ida Wright Sharpe

AGAIN. AND ALWAYS.

CONTENTS

*

ACKNOWLEDGMENTS

*

Both my sabbatical leave and the Tufts University Deans' Semester Research Leave gave me time and space away from teaching to finish the book. I am thankful for this. Thanks to Dean James Glaser for his help. Thanks to Dean Bárbara Brizuela and the Faculty Research Awards Committee for each providing funds to pay the permissions for many of the images that appear in this text. Thanks, as well, to former Dean Joanne Berger-Sweeney for her crucial early support of this work.

I had the good luck to present work from this project in a number of forums: Michigan State University; Extra(-ordinary) Presents, University of Erlangen, Germany; the Futures of Black Studies, University of Bremen, Germany; The Fleming Museum, University of Vermont; The Afrikan Black Coalition Conference, University of California, Irvine; University of Toronto; Cornell University; Caribbean Studies Association Conference; Black Folk in Dark Times, Vanderbilt University; American Studies Association Conference; Modern Language Association Conference; Southern Illinois University Edwardsville; Barnard College; Pratt Institute; Curatorial Controversies in Traumatic History and Pedagogy and Commemoration Seminar at York University, Toronto; the Dark Room Race and Visual Culture Seminar Panel, Black Portraiture(s) II: Imaging the Black Body and Re-Staging Histories, Florence, Italy; Black + Queer + Human Symposium, University of Toronto; The Black Studies Race Literacies Series, University of British Columbia, Vancouver, Canada. My thanks to the people who organized the panels and events at which I presented this work and to those people in attendance who so generously engaged the work-in-progress.

Earlier and substantially different portions of *In the Wake* appear in the following places: From "The Weather," the section on Barack Obama's speeches appears in an earlier but also much expanded form in "Three Scenes" in *On Marronage: Ethical Confrontations with Anti-Blackness* (2015), edited by P. Khalil Saucier and Tryon P. Woods (Trenton, NJ: Africa World Press, 131–153). The section in "The Hold" on Dasani Coates and William appears in a different form in the essay "Black Studies: In the Wake" in *The Black Scholar* 44, no. 2 (2014): 59–69.

The list of those who have accompanied and encouraged me is long. Any listing of them, and an alphabetical one at that, is incomplete, but it is a beginning. *Beloved*, Black Lives Matter, Black Youth Project 100, Nicholas Brady, Sabine Broeck, Kimberly Juanita Brown, Kimberly Nichele Brown, Kevin Browne, Tina Campt, David Chariandy, Margo Crawford, Warren Crichlow, Delia, Mario DiPaolantonia, Martin Donovan, Drana, "Dream Haiti," Lee Edelman, Andrea Fatona, Rafael Fonseca, Donette Francis, Vivek Freitas, Charlene Gilbert, Saidiya Hartman, Kimberly Hébert, Tiffany Willoughby Herard, Molly Hildebrand, Peter Hudson, Vijay Iyer, Aereile Jackson, Zakiyyah Iman Jackson, Amber Rose Johnson, Jessica Marie Johnson, Kima Jones, Aiyana Stanley-Jones, Mariame Kaba, Amor Kohli, Joseph Litvak, Lisa Lowe, Keguro Macharia, David Mann, *A Map to the Door of No Return: Notes to Belonging*, Egbert Alejandro Martina, Dianna McFadden, Katherine McKittrick, Diego Millan, Siddhartha Mitter, Fred Moten, John Murillo, Gee Ngugi, Tamara Nopper, Tavia Nyong'o, Abdi Osman, Jemima Pierre, Modhumita Roy, Ashraf Rushdy, Leslie Sanders, P. Khalil Saucier, Jared Sexton, Christopher Sharpe, Evie Shockley, Faith Smith, C. Riley Snorton, Eddy Souffrant, Hortense Spillers, Aparna Mishra Tarc, Grete Telander, Selamawit Terrefe, the unnamed Little Girl with the word *Ship* affixed to her forehead, "Venus in Two Acts," "Verso 55," Alex Weheliye, Frank Wilderson, Jaye Austin Williams, Jean Wu, Van Zimmerman, and *Zong!* To those whom I have inadvertently neglected to name here, I am no less thankful because of a temporary failure of memory.

After my sister IdaMarie died, Amor Kohli heard the unsaid and came to get me and he and Sonya cooked for me; Van Zimmerman was there through and in all of those wakes (and through some of his own) and I remain deeply grateful, my Tufts colleague Anne Gardulski generously met me for lunch to talk with me about water wakes and residence time; Kate Siklosi transcribed that interview with Anne and indexed the book; Abbe Schriber provided expert and timely help securing art and text permissions; Anthony Reed sent me parts of "Dream Haiti" as I waited for my book to arrive. Thank you.

At Duke University Press, thanks to Jade Brooks, Nicole Campbell, and Amy Buchanan. Most especially, thanks to Duke University Press editorial director Ken Wissoker for his kindness and his commitment to the work. Thanks, as well, to the two readers of my manuscript; what a privilege to be read so generously and well.

Dionne Brand and Rinaldo Walcott, thank you for reading, for your generative conversations with me, your clarity, insights, and for your being, in the wake.

ONE

The Wake

I wasn't there when my sister died. I was in Chicago at the Cultural Studies Association meeting and I was finishing the paper that was my first attempt at the work that became this book. My brother Christopher called on that Wednesday in May and asked if I was busy. I told him that I was finishing the paper I would give on Friday. He asked me to call him back when I was done. When two hours passed and I still hadn't called, he called me. He said that he'd wanted to wait but that our brother Stephen and sister Annette had urged him to call me back. They'd told him I would be upset if he waited. Our eldest sister Ida-Marie was dead, Christopher told me. There were very few other details. She lived alone. She was late to work. No more than ten minutes late, but she was always so prompt that ten minutes with no call, text, or email so alarmed her employers that they called the police and convinced them to go to her apartment. They found her there. I put the phone down. I called my partner and two friends. I texted one of my fellow presenters to tell him that I wouldn't be on the panel and why. I texted another friend, a former student who is now a professor at De-Paul University, and he said that he was coming to get me. He told me that I shouldn't be alone. I put down the phone and fell asleep.

That was May 2013 and I had no idea, then, that two more members of my family would also die within the next ten months. This would be the second time in my life when three immediate family members died in close succession. In the first instance, between February 2, 1997, January 19, 1998, and July 4, 1999, we survived the deaths of my nephew Jason Phillip Sharpe; my mother, Ida Wright Sharpe; and my eldest brother, Van Buren Sharpe III. As this deathly repetition appears here, it is one instantiation of the wake as the conceptual frame of and for living blackness in the diaspora in the still unfolding aftermaths of Atlantic chattel slavery.

No one was with my sister when she died at home less than a week after she, my brother Stephen, my sister Annette, and my brother-in-law James had returned from a ten-day vacation together in Florida. Her death was sudden and alarming. We still don't know what caused IdaMarie's death; the autopsy report was inconclusive.

IdaMarie and I weren't close. We had only ever had moments of closeness, like in the chiasmic aftermath of the death of her son, my nephew, Jason (figure 1.1). This lack of closeness was largely, though not only, because almost twenty-two years my senior we had never spent much time together, we had never really gotten to know each other, and I had grown used to her absence. I didn't, in fact, experience her absence *as* absence because when I was born she was already living in her own life, at a distance from me, because her relationship with our father was irretrievable, for reasons that remain unknown to me.

There are many silences in my family. I am the youngest of six children. My parents were born in Philadelphia in the first quarter of the twentieth century. My father, who went to Overbrook High School, was one of eight children and middle class (his mother had gone to Normal School in Washington, DC; three of my father's brothers went to Howard University), and my mother, who went to West Catholic Girls High School, was the only child of a working poor and single mother. My parents married on my mother's nineteenth birthday; my father was thirty. Neither of my parents went to college. My mother had always wanted to be an artist, but was told by the white nuns who were her teachers at West Catholic Girls that Black girls couldn't do that. So after graduating she trained to become certified as an X-ray technician. My father worked in the sorting room at the post office at Thirtieth Street in Philadelphia. My mother worked as an X-ray technician before I was born and then at TV *Guide* after she was diagnosed with and treated for cancer the first time. After that she worked at Sears, Roebuck, and Co., in St. Davids, Pennsylvania, in the garden department and then in the personnel department. We children went to Archbishop John Carroll High School, St. Katherine of Siena, the

Academy of Notre Dame de Namur, Devon Preparatory, and also Valley Forge Junior High School and Conestoga Senior High School; good-to-mediocre Catholic schools, elite private schools, and good public schools. We went there, that is, until the scholarship money ran out and/or the racism proved too much; sometimes the scholarship money ran out because of racism. In each of these private and public institutions and across generations (there were twenty-one and twenty-two years between my eldest siblings and me) we faced the kinds of racism, personal and institutional, that many people, across race, like to consign to the pre–*Brown v. Board of Education* southern United States. The overriding engine of US racism cut through my family's ambitions and desires. It coursed through our social and public encounters and our living room. Racism, the engine that drives the ship of state's national and imperial projects ("the American ship of state . . . the ark of the covenant that authorized both liberty and slavery": DeLoughrey 2010, 53) cuts through all of our lives and deaths inside and outside the nation, in the wake of its purposeful flow.

> *Wake: the track left on the water's surface by a ship; the disturbance caused by a body swimming or moved, in water; it is the air currents behind a body in flight; a region of disturbed flow.*[1]

In 1948 my parents moved with my two eldest siblings from West Philadelphia to Wayne, Pennsylvania, on the Main Line. They were Black working, middle-class, striving, people who lived at a four-way intersection, at one end of a small mixed-income Black neighborhood called Mt. Pleasant that was surrounded by largely upper-middle-class and wealthy white suburban neighborhoods (up the street were the St. David's Golf Club and the Valley Forge Military Academy). From what I understand, my parents moved to the suburbs for *opportunity*; they wanted what they both imagined and knew that they did not have and their children would not have access to in Philadelphia: from space for their children to grow (there would be six of us and the house was small), to a yard large enough to have fruit trees and a vegetable garden, to easier access to good educations for their children. (*Opportunity*: from the Latin *Ob-*, meaning "toward," and *portu(m)*, meaning "port": What is opportunity in the wake, and how is opportunity always framed?) This, of course, is not wholly, or even largely, a Black US phenomenon. This kind of movement happens all over the Black diaspora from and in the Caribbean and the continent to the metropole, the US great migrations of the early to mid-twentieth century that saw millions of Black people moving from the South to the North, and those people on the move in the contemporary from points all over the African continent to other points on the continent and also to Germany, Greece, Lampedusa.[2] Like many of these Black people on the move, my parents discovered that things were *not* better in this "new world": the subjections of constant and overt racism and isolation continued. After my father died when I was ten, we slid from lower-middle-class straitened circumstances into straight-up working poor. With all of the work that my parents did to try to enter and stay in the middle class, precarity and more than precarity remained. And after my father died, that precarity looked and felt like winters without heat because there was no money for oil; holes in ceilings, walls, and floors from water damage that we could not afford to repair; the fears and reality of electricity and other utilities being cut for nonpayment; fear of a lien being placed on the house because there was no, or not enough, money to pay property taxes. For my part, my dining services access was cut during my first semester in college, and after that semester the University of Pennsylvania almost did not allow me to return to campus because we were unable to pay the (small but too large for us) parental contribution. But through all of that and more, my mother tried to make a small path through the wake. She brought beauty into that house in every way that she could; she worked at joy, and she made livable moments, spaces, and places in the midst of all that was unlivable there, in the town we lived in; in the schools we attended; in the violence we saw and felt inside the home while my father was living and outside it in the larger white world before, during, and after his death. In other words, even as we experienced, recognized, and lived subjection, we did not *simply* or *only* live *in* subjection and *as* the subjected.[3] Though she was not part of any organized Black movements, except in how one's life and mind are organized by and positioned to apprehend the world through the optic of the door[4] and antiblackness, my mother was politically and socially astute. She was attuned not only to our individual circumstances but also to those circumstances as they were an indication of, and related to, the larger antiblack world that structured all of our lives. *Wake; the state of wakefulness; consciousness.* It was with this sense of wakefulness as consciousness that most of my family lived an awareness of itself as, and in, the wake of the unfinished project of emancipation.[5]

> *So, the same set of questions and issues are presenting themselves to us across these historical periods. It [is] the same story that is telling itself, but through the different technologies and processes of that particular period.* (Saunders 2008a, 67)

It is a big leap from working class, to Ivy League schools, to being a tenured professor. And *a part of* that leap and *apart from* its specificities are the sense and awareness of precarity; the precarities of the afterlives of slavery ("skewed life chances, limited access to health and education, premature death, incarceration, and impoverishment": Hartman 2007, 6); the precarities of the ongoing disaster of the ruptures of chattel slavery. They texture my reading practices, my ways of being in and of the world, my relations with and to others. Here's Maurice Blanchot (1995, 1–2): "The disaster ruins everything, all the while leaving everything intact. . . . When the disaster comes upon us, it does not come. The disaster is its imminence, but since the future, as we conceive of it in the order of lived time belongs to the disaster, the disaster has always already withdrawn or dissuaded it; there is no future for the disaster, just as there is no time or space for its accomplishment."[6] Transatlantic slavery was and is the disaster. The disaster of Black subjection was and *is* planned; terror is disaster and "terror has a history" (Youngquist 2011, 7) and it is deeply atemporal. The history of capital is inextricable from the history of Atlantic chattel slavery. The disaster and the writing of disaster are never present, are always present.[7] In this work, *In the Wake: On Blackness and Being,* I want to think "the wake" as a problem of and for thought. I want to think "care" as a problem for thought. I want to think care in the wake as a problem for thinking and of and for Black non/being in the world.[8] Put another way, *In the Wake: On Blackness and Being* is a work that insists and performs that thinking needs care ("all thought is Black thought")[9] and that thinking and care need to stay in the wake.

December 2013. I was in the grocery store when my brother Stephen called. I listened to the message and I called him back immediately. The tone of his voice and the fact of the call let me know that something was wrong because in recent years my brother became very bad at making and returning calls, a fact that he was always deeply apologetic about. When he answered the phone, he told me that he had bad news about Annette. I froze. Asked, "What? Is she okay?" Stephen told me yes, physically she was okay, but Annette and my brother-in-law James's adopted and estranged son Caleb (called Trey before he was adopted and renamed) had been murdered in Pittsburgh. Stephen had no other information.

Caleb had been severely abused before he was adopted at the age of five. He was very small for his age and quiet, and my sister and brother-in-law at first were not aware of the extent or the severity of the abuse he had suffered. But when Caleb continued to have trouble adjusting, they sought the help of therapists. In response to a therapist's question about the difficulties he was facing, the then six-year-old Caleb replied, "I'm just bad." Eventually Caleb was diagnosed with a severe attachment disorder, which meant that it was likely he would never bond with my sister. There are other stories to be told here; they are not mine to tell.

I put my basket down and left the store. When I got home I searched online for Caleb's name, and the brief news stories I found on the websites of the *Pittsburgh Post-Gazette* and the *TribLive* were about the murder of a twenty-year-old young Black man on Pittsburgh's North Side, and together they provided all of the details I had of my nephew's death.[10] "Caleb Williams, a twenty-year-old Black male from Turtle Creek, was fatally shot to death in the trunk and neck as he and another person left an apartment in the 1700 block of Letsche Street in the North Side. Shots were fired from an adjoining apartment. He was taken to Allegheny General Hospital, where he later died. No one has been charged; the investigation is ongoing."[11]

This wasn't the first time that I searched newspapers for the details of a murdered family member. In 1994 the Philadelphia police murdered my cousin Robert, who was schizophrenic; he had become schizophrenic after his first year as an undergraduate at the University of Pennsylvania. What I have been able to reconstruct with the help of my brother Christopher, my partner, memory, and online news archives is that Robert was living in an apartment in Germantown not far from my uncle, his father, and my aunt, his stepmother, and he had stopped taking his medication. He was a big man, six foot eight. Apparently he was agitated and had been walking the neighborhood. "A Germantown man was shot and killed last night when he ended an eight-hour stand-off with police by walking out of his apartment building and pointing a starter pistol at officers, police said. Robert Sharpe, forty, was shot several times outside the apartment building on Manheim Street near Wayne Avenue. He was pronounced dead a short time later at Medical College of Pennsylvania Hospital's main campus" (Taylor 1994).

What the paper did not say is that Robert's neighbors knew him and were not afraid of him; they were concerned for him and they wanted help calming his agitation. What the paper did not say is that the police shot Robert, who was unarmed, or armed with a starter pistol — a toy gun — point blank eleven times, or nineteen times, in the back.[12] There was no seeking justice here. What would justice mean?[13] Joy James and João Costa Vargas ask in "Refusing Blackness-as-Victimization: Tray-von Martin and the Black Cyborgs": "What happens when instead of becoming enraged and shocked every time a Black person is killed in the United States, we recognize Black death as a predictable and con-stitutive aspect of this democracy? What will happen then if instead of demanding justice we recognize (or at least consider) that the very notion of justice . . . produces and requires Black exclusion and death as normative" (James and Costa Vargas 2012, 193). The ongoing state-sanctioned legal and extralegal murders of Black people are normative and, for this so-called democracy, necessary; it is the ground we walk on. And that it *is* the ground lays out that, and perhaps how, we might begin to live in relation to this requirement for our death. What kinds of possibilities for rupture might be opened up? What happens when we proceed as if we *know* this, antiblackness, to be the ground on which we stand, the ground from which we to attempt to speak, for instance, an "I" or a "we" who know, an "I" or a "we" who care?

That these and other Black deaths are produced as normative still leaves gaps and unanswered questions for those of us in the wake of those specific and cumulative deaths. My niece Dianna sent me a video about her cousin, my nephew. It was dedicated to "Little Nigga Trey," and that the video exists speaks to my nephew's life after he relocated and returned to live with and in proximity to his birth family in Pitts-burgh and also speaks to the nonbiological family he made as a young adult.[14] Caleb's life was singular and difficult, and it was also not dis-similar to the lives of many young Black people living in, and produced by, the contemporary conditions of Black life as it is lived near death, as deathliness, in the wake of slavery. "The U.S. Marshals this morning arrested a Pittsburgh homicide suspect in New Kensington who has been on the loose since December. ███████████ is charged with killing Caleb Williams, 20, of Turtle Creek on Dec. 10."[15] *Wake; in the line of recoil of (a gun).*

I include the personal here to connect the social forces on a specific, particular family's being in the wake to those of all Black people in the wake; to mourn and to illustrate the ways our individual lives are always swept up in the wake produced and determined, though not absolutely, by the afterlives of slavery. Put another way, I include the personal here in order to position this work, and myself, in and of the wake. The "autobiographical example," says Saidiya Hartman, "is not a personal story that folds onto itself; it's not about navel gazing, it's really about trying to look at historical and social process and one's own formation as a window onto social and historical processes, as an example of them" (Saunders 2008b, 7). Like Hartman I include the personal here, "to tell a story capable of engaging and countering the violence of abstraction" (Hartman 2008, 7).

Late January 2014. I was preparing to go to Germany to give a talk the first week of February when my niece Dianna, the daughter of my eldest brother Van Buren, called to tell me that Stephen, my second oldest brother, was ill and that she and Karen, my sister-in-law, had called an ambulance to take him to the hospital (figure 1.2). She said he didn't want to go but that he was having difficulty breathing. I knew that Stephen hadn't been well. At IdaMarie's funeral he seemed and looked aged and in pain. I made myself believe that what I was seeing on his face and body were "just" (as if this could be "just" in any meaning of the word) the long-term effects of sickle cell, his deep depression over IdaMarie's death, and the grinding down of poverty—the poverty of the work-too-hard-and-still-can't-make-ends-meet kind. Then I simultaneously thought, *but didn't want to think*, that he was really ill. Now, panicked, I asked Dianna if I should come. When she said no, I told her that I was headed to Germany in a few days and that I would cancel that trip in order to be there; I told her I wanted to see Stephen, wanted to be with him.

The next day I talked to Stephen, and with his assurances I made the trip to Bremen, Germany, where I was to give a talk at the University of Bremen, titled "In the Wake." This was the third iteration of the work that has become this book. In our conversation Stephen told me that he was weak and worried and that the doctors weren't sure what was wrong with him. There were many tests and multiple and conflicting diagnoses.

In the days after I returned from Bremen the doctors finally gave Stephen a diagnosis of malignant mesothelioma. They told him that he likely had between six and nine months to live. We were devastated. None of us were sure how he got this rare cancer that is usually caused by exposure to asbestos. We learned from the doctors that the dormancy period for mesotheliomas is long, from ten to fifty years. If this mesothelioma was from what and from where we thought, we were struck that the damage from one summer's work forty-five years earlier at a local insulation company in Wayne, Pennsylvania, when he was fourteen years old could suddenly appear, now, to fracture the present. In the wake, the past that is not past reappears, always, to rupture the present.

The Past — or, more accurately, pastness — is a position. Thus, in no way can we identify the past as past. (Trouillot 1997, 15)

In one of the moments that Stephen was alone in his hospital room, before he was moved to a rehabilitation center, then back to the intensive care unit at the hospital, and finally to hospice care, he called me and asked me to do him a favor. He said he knew he could count on me. He asked me to not let him suffer; to make sure that he was medicated enough that he wouldn't suffer. I told him yes, I would do that. We knew that for each of us the unspoken end of that sentence was "the way our mother did" as she was dying of cancer (figure 1.3).

Several nights later Dianna called and told me to come quickly. We rented a car and drove from Cambridge, Massachusetts, to Norristown, Pennsylvania. But my brother was no longer able to speak by the time we got to the hospital, in a repetition of 1998, when I made it to my mother's side from Geneva, New York, where I was teaching in my first job as I completed my PhD dissertation. But I was there. He registered my presence. (I am the youngest child. We were always there for each other.) I could speak with him. I could hold his hand, and stroke his face, and play Stevie Wonder and Bob Marley. I could tell him how much I loved him, how much he would live on in my life, and in the lives of everyone he had touched.

February 21, 2014. My sister Annette and her husband James had just left Stephen's hospital hospice room, and more of Stephen's friends started arriving; they were coming in from Texas and California and other states far from Pennsylvania. My youngest brother, Christopher (he is five years older than I), was traveling the next day from California. My partner and I bought wine and food. We brought it back to the hospital room. Several of Stephen's friends arrived. We opened the wine, we talked and laughed, we toasted his life. As we gathered around Stephen's bed and shared stories, played music, laughed, and told him how much we loved him, suddenly Stephen sat up, he looked at us, he tried to speak, a tear ran down his face, he exhaled, he lay back down, and he died. *Wake: a watch or vigil held beside the body of someone who has died, sometimes accompanied by ritual observances including eating and drinking.*

Defend the dead. (Philip 2008, 26)

What does it mean to defend the dead? To tend to the Black dead and dying: to tend to the Black person, to Black people, always living in the push toward our death? It means work. It is work: hard emotional, physical, and intellectual work that demands vigilant attendance to the needs of the dying, to ease their way, and also to the needs of the living. Vigilance, too, because any- and everywhere we are, medical and other professionals treat Black patients differently: often they don't listen to the concerns of patients and their families; they ration palliative medicine, or deny them access to it altogether. While there are multiple reasons for this (Stein 2007),[16] experience and research tell us "'people assume that, relative to whites, blacks feel less pain because they have faced more hardship.' . . . Because they are believed to be less sensitive to pain, black people are forced to endure more pain" (Silverstein 2013).[17] We had to work to make sure that Stephen was as comfortable as possible.

Being with Stephen and other family and friends of Stephen's as he died, I *re*-experienced the power of the wake. The power of and in sitting with someone as they die, the important work of sitting (together) in the pain and sorrow of death as a way of marking, remembering, and celebrating a life. *Wake: grief, celebration, memory, and those among the living who, through ritual, mourn their passing and celebrate their life in particular the watching of relatives and friends beside the body of the dead person from death to burial and the drinking, feasting, and other observances incidental to this.* The wake continued after Stephen's death, to the funeral, and then into the gathering and celebration of his life afterward.

And while the wake produces Black death and trauma—"violence … precedes and exceeds Blacks" (Wilderson 2010, 76)—we, Black people everywhere and anywhere we are, still produce in, into, and through the wake an insistence on existing: we insist Black being into the wake.

On Existence in the Wake/Teaching in the Wake

I teach a course called Memory for Forgetting. The title came from my misremembering the title of a book that Judith Butler mentioned in an MLA talk on activism and the academy in San Diego in 2004. The book was Mahmoud Darwish's *Memory for Forgetfulness*, and the course looks at two traumatic histories (the Holocaust and largely US/North American slavery) and the film, memoir, narrative, literature, and art that take up these traumas. I have found that I have had to work very hard with students when it comes to thinking through slavery and its afterlives. When I taught the course chronologically, I found that many, certainly well-meaning, students held onto whatever empathy they might have for reading about the Holocaust but not for North American slavery. After two semesters of this, I started teaching the Holocaust first and then North American chattel slavery. But even after I made the change, students would say things about the formerly enslaved like, "Well, they were *given* food and clothing; there was a kind of care there. And what would the enslaved have done otherwise?" The "otherwise" here means: What lives would Black people have had outside of slavery? How would they have survived independent of those who enslaved them? In order for the students in the class to confront their inability to think blackness otherwise and to think slavery as state violence, at a certain moment in the course I replay a scene from Claude Lanzmann's *Shoah*. The scene is in the section of *Shoah* where we meet Simon Srebnik (one of three survivors of the massacre at Chelmno then living in Israel) on his return to Chelmno, Poland. In this scene Srebnik is surrounded by the townspeople who remember him as the young boy with the beautiful voice who was forced by the Germans to sing on the river every morning. At first the townspeople are glad to see him, glad to know that he is alive. Soon, though, and with ease, their relief and astonishment turn into something else, and they begin to speak about how they helped the Jewish residents of Chelmno, and then they begin to blame the Jews of Chelmno for their own murder. The camera stays on Srebnik's face, as it becomes more and more frozen into a kind of smile as these people surround him. Some of these people who are brought out of their homes by his singing on the river—as if he is a revenant—are the very people who by apathy or more directly abetted the murder of thousands of the town's Jewish residents. The students are appalled by all of this. They feel for him. I ask them if they can imagine if, after the war's end, Simon Srebnik had no place to go other than to return to this country and this town; to these people who would have also seen him dead; who had, in fact, tried to kill him and every other Jewish person in Chelmno. That is, I say, the condition in the post–Civil War United States of the formerly enslaved and their descendants; still on the plantation, still surrounded by those who claimed ownership over them and who fought, and fight still, to extend that state of capture and subjection in as many legal and extralegal ways as possible, into the present. The means and modes of Black subjection may have changed, but the fact and structure of that subjection remain.

Those of us who teach, write, and think about slavery and its afterlives encounter myriad silences and ruptures in time, space, history, ethics, research, and method as we do our work. Again and again scholars of slavery face absences in the archives as we attempt to find "the agents buried beneath" (Spillers 2003b) the accumulated erasures, projections, fabulations, and misnamings. There are, I think, specific ways that Black scholars of slavery get wedged in the partial truths of the archives while trying to make sense of their silences, absences, and modes of dis/appearance. The methods most readily available to us sometimes, oftentimes, force us into positions that run counter to what we know. That is, our knowledge, of slavery and Black being in slavery, is gained from our studies, yes, but also in excess of those studies;[18] it is gained through the kinds of knowledge from and of the everyday, from what Dionne Brand calls "sitting in the room with history."[19] We are expected to discard, discount, disregard, jettison, abandon, and measure those ways of knowing and to enact epistemic violence that we know to be violence against others and ourselves. In other words, for Black academics to produce legible work in the academy often means adhering to research methods that are "drafted into the service of a larger destructive force" (Saunders 2008a, 67), thereby doing violence to our own capacities to read, think, and imagine otherwise. Despite knowing otherwise, we are often disciplined into thinking through and along lines that reinscribe our own annihilation, reinforcing and reproducing what Sylvia Wynter (1994, 70) has called our "narratively condemned status." We must become undisciplined. The work we do requires new modes and methods of research and teaching; new ways of entering and leaving the archives of slavery, of undoing the "racial calculus and . . . political arithmetic that were entrenched centuries ago" (Hartman 2008, 6) and that live into the present. I think this is what Brand describes in *A Map to the Door of No Return* as a kind of blackened knowledge, an unscientific method, that comes from observing that where one stands is relative to the door of no return and that moment of historical and ongoing rupture. With this as the ground, I've been trying to articulate a method of encountering a past that is not past. A method along the lines of a sitting with, a gathering, and a tracking of phenomena that disproportionately and devastatingly affect Black peoples any and everywhere we are. I've been thinking of this gathering, this collecting and reading toward a new analytic, as the wake and wake work, and I am interested in plotting, mapping, and collecting the archives of the everyday of Black immanent and imminent death, and in tracking the ways we resist, rupture, and disrupt that immanence and imminence aesthetically and materially.

I am interested in how we imagine ways of knowing that past, in excess of the fictions of the archive, but not only that. I am interested, too, in the ways we recognize the many manifestations of that fiction and that excess, that past not yet past, in the present.

In the Wake

Keeping each of the definitions of wake in mind, I want to think and argue for one aspect of Black being in the wake as consciousness and to propose that to be *in* the wake is to occupy and to be occupied by the continuous and changing present of slavery's as yet unresolved unfolding. *To be* "in" the wake, to occupy that grammar, the infinitive, might provide another way of theorizing, in/for/from what Frank Wilderson refers to as "stay[ing] in the hold of the ship."[20] With each of those definitions of wake present throughout my text, I argue that rather than seeking a resolution to blackness's ongoing and irresolvable abjection, one might approach Black being in the wake as a form of *consciousness*. Political scientists, historians, philosophers, literary scholars, and others have posed as a question for thought the endurance of racial inequality after juridical emancipation and civil rights, and they have interrogated the conflation of blackness as the ontological negation of being with Black subjects and communities. That is, across disciplines, scholars and researchers continue to be concerned with the endurance of antiblackness in and outside the contemporary. In that way *In the Wake: On Blackness and Being* joins the work of those scholars who investigate the ongoing problem of Black exclusion from social, political, and cultural belonging; our abjection from the realm of the human. But the book departs from those scholars and those works that look for political, juridical, or even philosophical answers to this problem. My project looks instead to current quotidian disasters in order to ask what, if anything, survives this insistent Black exclusion, this ontological negation, and how do literature, performance, and visual culture observe and mediate this un/survival. To do this work of staying in the wake and to perform wake work I look also to forms of Black expressive culture (like the works of poets and poet-novelists M. NourbeSe Philip, Dionne Brand, and Kamau Brathwaite) that do not seek to explain or resolve the question of this exclusion in terms of assimilation, inclusion, or civil or human rights, but rather depict aesthetically the impossibility of such resolutions by representing the paradoxes of blackness within and after the legacies of slavery's denial of Black humanity. I name this paradox the wake, and I use the wake in all of its meanings as a means of understanding how slavery's violences emerge within the contemporary conditions of spatial, legal, psychic, material, and other dimensions of Black non/being as well as in Black modes of resistance.

> *If slavery persists as an issue in the political life of black America,*
> *it is not because of an antiquarian obsession with bygone days*
> *or the burden of a too-long memory, but because black lives are*

still imperiled and devalued by a racial calculus and a political
arithmetic that were entrenched centuries ago. This is the afterlife of
slavery—skewed life chances, limited access to health and education,
premature death, incarceration, and impoverishment. I, too, am the
afterlife of slavery. (Hartman 2007, 6)

Living in/the wake of slavery is living "the afterlife of property" and living the afterlife of *partus sequitur ventrem* (that which is brought forth follows the womb), in which the Black child inherits the non/ status, the non/being of the mother. That inheritance of a non/status is everywhere apparent *now* in the ongoing criminalization of Black women and children. Living in the wake on a global level means living the disastrous time and effects of continued marked migrations, Mediterranean and Caribbean disasters, trans-American and -African migration, structural adjustment imposed by the International Monetary Fund that continues imperialisms/colonialisms, and more. And here, in the United States, it means living and dying through the policies of the first US Black president; it means the gratuitous violence of stop-and-frisk and Operation Clean Halls; rates of Black incarceration that boggle the mind (Black people represent 60 percent of the imprisoned population); the immanence of death as "a predictable and constitutive aspect of *this* democracy" (James and Costa Vargas 2012, 193, emphasis mine). Living in the wake means living the history and present of terror, from slavery to the present, as the ground of our everyday Black existence; living the historically and geographically dis/continuous but always present and endlessly reinvigorated brutality in, and on, our bodies while even as that terror is visited on our bodies the realities of that terror are erased. Put another way, living in the wake means living in and with terror in that in much of what passes for public discourse *about* terror we, Black people, become the *carriers* of terror, terror's embodiment, and not the primary objects of terror's multiple enactments; the ground of terror's possibility globally. This is everywhere clear as we think about those Black people in the United States who can "weaponize sidewalks" (Trayvon Martin) and shoot themselves while handcuffed (Victor White III, Chavis Carter, Jesus Huerta, and more), those Black people transmigrating[21] the African continent toward the Mediterranean and then to Europe who are imagined as insects, swarms, vectors of disease; familiar narratives of danger and disaster that attach to our always already weaponized Black bodies (the weapon is blackness). We must also, for example, think of President Obama's former press secretary Robert Gibbs, who said, commenting on the drone murder of sixteen-year-old US citizen Abdulrahman Al-Alwaki, "I would suggest that you should have a far more responsible father if you are truly concerned about the well being [*sic*] of your children" (Grim 2012).[22] We must consider this alongside the tracking of Haitians and Dominicans of Haitian descent without papers by drones in the midst of the ongoing ethnic cleansing in the Dominican Republic.[23] We must consider Gibbs's statement alongside Barack Obama's reprimands of Black men in the United States, his admonishing them to be responsible fathers. Consider, too, the resurgence of narratives that Black people were better off in chattel slavery. This is Black life in the wake; this is the flesh, these are bodies, to which anything and everything can be and is done.

In the immediate aftermath of the June 17, 2015, murders of six Black women and three Black men in the Emanuel African Methodist Episcopal (AME) Church in South Carolina in the United States, the poet Claudia Rankine published a *New York Times* op-ed piece titled "The Condition of Black Life Is One of Mourning." Rankine writes, "Though the white liberal imagination likes to feel temporarily bad about black suffering, there really is no mode of empathy that can replicate the daily strain of knowing that as a black person you can be killed for simply being black: no hands in your pockets, no playing music, no sudden movements, no driving your car, no walking at night, no walking in the day, no turning onto this street, no entering this building, no standing your ground, no standing here, no standing there, no talking back, no playing with toy guns, no living while black" (Rankine 2015). To be in the wake is to live in those no's, to live in the no-space that the law is not bound to respect, to live in no citizenship, to live in the long time of Dred and Harriet Scott; and it is more than that. To be/in the wake is to occupy that time/space/place/construction (being in the wake) in all of the meanings I referenced. To be in the wake is to recognize the categories I theorize in this text as the ongoing locations of Black being: the wake, the ship, the hold, and the weather. To be in the wake is also to recognize the ways that we are constituted through and by continued vulnerability to overwhelming force though not *only* known to ourselves and to each other *by* that force.[24]

In the midst of so much death and the fact of Black life as proximate to death, how do we attend to physical, social, and figurative death and also to the largeness that is Black life, Black life insisted from death? I want to suggest that that might look something like wake work.

Wake Work

When I finally arrived at the door of no return, there was an official there, a guide who was either a man in his ordinary life or an idiot or a dissembler. But even if he was a man in his ordinary life or an idiot or a dissembler, he was authoritative. Exhausted violet, the clerk interjects. Yes he was says the author, violet snares. For some strange reason he wanted to control the story. Violet files. Violet chemistry. Violet unction. It was December, we had brought a bottle of rum, some ancient ritual we remembered from nowhere and no one. We stepped one behind the other as usual. The castle was huge, opulent, a going concern in its time. We went like pilgrims. You were pilgrims. We were pilgrims. This is the holiest we ever were. Our gods were in the holding cells. We awakened our gods and we left them there, because we never needed gods again. We did not have wicked gods so they understood. They lay in their corners, on their disintegrated floors, they lay on their wall of skin dust. They stood when we entered, happy to see us. Our guide said, this was the prison cell for the men, this was the prison cell for the women. I wanted to strangle the guide as if he were the original guide. It took all my will. Yet in the rooms the guide was irrelevant, the gods woke up and we felt pity for them, and affection and love; they felt happy for us, we were still alive. Yes, we are still alive we said. And we had returned to thank them. You are still alive, they said. Yes we are still alive. They looked at us like violet; like violet teas they drank us. We said here we are. They said, you are still alive. We said, yes, yes we are still alive. How lemon, they said, how blue like fortune. We took the bottle of rum from our veins, we washed their faces. We were pilgrims, they were gods. We sewed the rim of their skins with cotton. This is what we had. They said with wonder and admiration, you are still alive, like hydrogen, like oxygen.

We all stood there for some infinite time. We did weep, but that is nothing in comparison.

—Dionne Brand, *Verso 55*

If, as I have so far suggested, we think the metaphor of the wake in the entirety of its meanings (the keeping watch with the dead, the path of a ship, a consequence of something, in the line of flight and/or sight, awakening, and consciousness) and we join the wake with work in order that we might make the wake and *wake work* our analytic, we might continue to imagine new ways to live in the wake of slavery, in slavery's afterlives, to survive (and more) the afterlife of property. In short, I mean wake work to be a mode of inhabiting *and* rupturing this episteme with our known lived and un/imaginable lives. With that analytic we might imagine otherwise from what we know *now* in the wake of slavery.

Dionne Brand does this wake work as she imagines otherwise in *Verso 55*, a verso in which she not only revisits A *Map to the Door of No Return*'s imagining of diaspora consciousness's relation to that door as mythic and real location but also imagines an encounter between the returned from diaspora and those who were held in the cells of the forts.[25] She imagines those who were held, reconfiguring—coming back together in wonder—the traces of their former selves rising up in greeting. Here the ancestors are like Marie Ursule, who, in *At the Full and Change of the Moon*, reanimates those Ursuline nuns who were her enslavers for the purpose of looking after her daughter Bola whom she dreams into a, into the, future. In *Verso 55*, Brand imagines that with the entrance of the pilgrims those who were held reconstitute from where they "lay in their corners, on their disintegrated floors, they lay on their wall of skin dust," and stand to greet them; the ancestors, the only gods we had, their traces so much dust and haunt in those holding rooms. With these words Brand produces into the wake *other than* the "production of nothing—empty rooms, and silence, and lives reduced to waste"; she imagines other uses for "the scraps of the archive" (Hartman 2008, 4).[26] Brand, like Hartman, encounters these rooms, this pain of and in the archive, but those rooms are not empty, and though the scraps of cotton, new world slave crop, may in fact be insufficient to our needs and to theirs, they are what we have to offer. And those dwellers of the rooms who had no thoughts of visitors, could not know, but might imagine, that anything, any part, of them would survive the holding, the shipping, the water, and the weather, drink those visitors in like violet tea and lemon air. *Verso 55* is filled with the knowledge that this holding, these deaths, that shipping ought never to have happened, and with that knowledge and "the scraps of the archive" Brand imagines something that feels completely new. The rooms are not empty and the scraps are what we have to offer.

But even if those Africans who were in the holds, who left something of their prior selves in those rooms as a trace to be discovered, and who passed through the doors of no return did not survive the holding and the sea, they, like us, are alive in hydrogen, in oxygen; in carbon, in phosphorous, and iron; in sodium and chlorine. This is what we know about those Africans thrown, jumped, dumped overboard in Middle Passage; they are with us still, in the time of the wake, known as residence time.

They said with wonder and admiration, you are still alive, like hydrogen, like oxygen. (Brand 2015)

Brand does this in *A Map to the Door of No Return* as well, particularly with her "Ruttier for the Marooned in Diaspora," which bristles with her refusal to think return, her dislodging of belonging, and her *hard insisting* on the facts of displacement and the living in and as the displaced of diaspora. NourbeSe Philip does this in *Zong!* through her destruction of the archive in order to tell "the story that cannot be told" but must still be told (Saunders 2008a, 65). We must be (and we already are) about the work of what I am calling wake work as a theory and praxis of the wake; a theory and a praxis of Black being in diaspora.

I am trying to find the language for this work, find the form for this work. Language and form fracture more every day. I am trying, too, to find the words that will articulate care and the words to think what Keguro Macharia (2015) calls those "we formations." I am trying to think how to perform the labor of them. Or what Tinsley (2008, 191) calls a "feeling and a feeling for" and what Glissant ([1995] 2006, 9) refers to as "knowing ourselves as part and as crowd." This is what I am calling wake work. With Brand and Philip, I want to sound this language anew, sound a new language. Thinking, still, with Brand and Philip, who demand, always, a new thinking, I want to distinguish what I am calling Black being in the wake and wake work from the work of melancholia and mourning.[27] And though wake work is, at least in part, attentive to mourning and the mourning work that takes place on local and trans*local and global levels, and even as we know that mourning an event might be interminable, how does one mourn the interminable event? Just as wake work troubles mourning, so too do the wake and wake work trouble the ways most museums and memorials take up trauma and memory. That is, if museums and memorials materialize a kind of reparation (repair) and enact their own pedagogies as they position visitors to have a particular experience or set of experiences about an event that is seen to be past, how does one memorialize chattel slavery and its afterlives, which are unfolding still? How do we memorialize an event that is still ongoing? Might we instead understand the absence of a National Slavery Museum in the United States as recognition of the ongoingness of the conditions of capture? Because how does one memorialize the everyday? How does one, in the words so often used by such institutions, "come to terms with" (which usually means move past) ongoing and quotidian atrocity? Put another way, I'm interested in ways of seeing and imagining responses to terror in the varied and various ways that our Black lives are lived under occupation; ways that attest to the modalities of Black life lived in, as, under, and despite Black death. And I want to think about what this imagining calls forth, to think through what it calls on "us" to do, think, feel in the wake of slavery—which is to say in an ongoing present of subjection and resistance; which is to say wake work, wake theory. I want, too, to distinguish what I am calling and calling for as care from state-imposed regimes of surveillance.[28] How can we think (and rethink and rethink) care laterally, in the register of the intramural, in a different relation than that of the violence of the state? In what ways do we remember the dead, those lost in the Middle Passage, those who arrived reluctantly, and those still arriving? To quote Gaston Bachelard, whom I arrived at through Elizabeth DeLoughrey's "Heavy Waters," "water is an element 'which remembers the dead'" (DeLoughrey 2010, 704).

What, then, are the ongoing coordinates and effects of the wake, and what does it mean to *inhabit* that Fanonian "zone of non-Being" within and after slavery's denial of Black humanity?[29] Inhabiting here is the state of being inhabited/occupied and also being or dwelling in. In activating the multiple registers of "wake," I have turned to images, poetry, and literature that take up the wake as a way toward understanding how slavery's continued unfolding is constitutive of the contemporary conditions of spatial, legal, psychic, and material dimensions of Black non/being as well as Black aesthetic and other modes of deformation and interruption. That set of work by Black artists, poets, writers, and thinkers is positioned against a set of quotidian catastrophic events and their reporting that together comprise what I am calling the orthography of the wake. The latter is a dysgraphia of disaster, and these disasters arrive by way of the rapid, deliberate, repetitive, and wide circulation on television and social media of Black social, material, and psychic death. This orthography makes domination in/visible and not/visceral. This orthography is an instance of what I am calling the Weather; it registers and produces the conventions of antiblackness in the present and into the future.

A reprise and an elaboration: Wakes are processes; through them we think about the dead and about our relations to them; they are rituals through which to enact grief and memory. Wakes allow those among the living to mourn the passing of the dead through ritual; they are the watching of relatives and friends beside the body of the deceased from death to burial and the accompanying drinking, feasting, and other observances, a watching practiced as a religious observance. But wakes are also "the track left on the water's surface by a ship (figure 1.4); the disturbance caused by a body swimming, or one that is moved, in water; the air currents behind a body in flight; a region of disturbed flow; in the line of sight of (an observed object); and (something) in the line of recoil of (a gun)"; finally, wake means being awake and, also, consciousness.

In the wake, the semiotics of the slave ship continue: from the forced movements of the enslaved to the forced movements of the migrant and the refugee, to the regulation of Black people in North American streets and neighborhoods, to those ongoing crossings of and drownings in the Mediterranean Sea, to the brutal colonial reimaginings of the slave ship and the ark; to the reappearances of the slave ship in everyday life in the form of the prison, the camp, and the school.

As we go about wake work, we must think through containment, regulation, punishment, capture, and captivity and the ways the manifold representations of blackness become the symbol, par excellence, for the less-than-human being condemned to death. We must think about Black flesh, Black optics, and ways of producing enfleshed work; think the ways the hold cannot and does not hold even as the hold remains in the form of the semiotics of the slave ship hold, the prison, the womb, and elsewhere in and as the tension between being and instrumentality that is Black being in the wake. At stake is not recognizing antiblackness as total climate. At stake, too, is not recognizing an insistent Black visualsonic resistance to that imposition of non/being. How might we stay in the wake with and as those whom the state positions to die ungrievable deaths and live lives meant to be unlivable? These are questions of temporality, the *longue durée*, the residence and hold time of the wake. At stake, then is to stay in this wake time toward inhabiting a blackened consciousness that would rupture the structural silences produced and facilitated by, and that produce and facilitate, Black social and physical death.

For, if we are lucky, we live in the knowledge that the wake has positioned us as no-citizen.[30] If we are lucky, the knowledge of this positioning avails us particular ways of re/seeing, re/inhabiting, and re/imagining the world. And we might use these ways of being in the wake in our responses to terror and the varied and various ways that our Black lives are lived under occupation. I want *In the Wake* to declare that we are Black peoples in the wake with no state or nation to protect us, with no citizenship bound to be respected, and to position us in the modalities of Black life lived in, as, under, despite Black death: to think and be and act from there. It is my particular hope that the praxis of the wake and wake work, the theory and performance of the wake and wake work, as modes of attending to Black life and Black suffering, are imagined and performed here with enough specificity to attend to the direness of the multiple and overlapping presents that we face; it is also my hope that the praxis of the wake and wake work might have enough capaciousness to travel and do work that I have not here been able to imagine or anticipate.

1.1 The author (age ten) and her nephew Jason Phillip Sharpe (age approximately one month). **1.2** Stephen Wheatley Sharpe (age eighteen). **1.3** Ida Wright Sharpe (my mother), Van Buren Sharpe Jr. (my father), IdaMarie Sharpe (my sister), Van Buren Sharpe III (my brother), and Stephen Wheatley Sharpe (infant; my brother) in 1954. Everyone in this photograph is now dead.

1.4 The wake of a cruise ship on the open ocean. Photo taken on March 10, 2011.
© Bcbounders | Dreamstime.com — Cruise Ship Wake Photo

TWO

The Ship

*The Trans*Atlantic*

who could not see this like the passage's continuum
—Dionne Brand, Ossuary XI, *Ossuaries*
(on Jacob Lawrence's *Shipping Out*, part of his *War* series)

Allan Sekula and Noël Burch's *The Forgotten Space—A Film Essay Seeking to Understand the Contemporary Maritime World in Relation to the Symbolic Legacy of the Sea* (2010) is a film that follows the movement of shipping containers on land and sea; it is a film about global capital and the wreckage it leaves in the wake. The filmmakers "visit displaced farmers and villagers in Holland and Belgium, underpaid truck drivers in Los Angeles, seafarers aboard mega-ships shuttling between Asia and Europe, and factory workers in China," and finally the Guggenheim Museum in Bilbao, where they "discover the most sophisticated expression of the belief that the maritime economy, and the sea itself, is somehow obsolete."[1] Burch and Sekula write in *New Left Review*, "The subject of the film is globalization and the sea, the 'forgotten space' of our modernity. *Its premise is that the oceans remain the crucial space of globalization: nowhere else is the disorientation, violence and alienation of contemporary capitalism more manifest*" (Burch and Sekula 2011; emphasis mine). The filmmakers say the film is about a system. With such a premise, surely a film on the voraciousness of capital, the capitalization of human misery, and the profits of immiseration would contend, even tangentially, with the Middle Passage, the shipped, and with that fleshly wreckage that capital wrought. *The Forgotten Space* is indebted to an earlier Sekula work, a book titled *Fish Story*, which consists of nine chapters. Chapter 3 of *Fish Story* is titled "Middle Passage," and one might expect that as it locates its subject in and as the ocean, the shipping industry, and ports, the images and text of that chapter would contend with the historical Middle Passage and slavery. And perhaps, given the title, chapter 3 might also have addressed that always present throwing and jumping overboard, and the fish that fed and feed on those bodies in the wake of the ships.[2] Though the long essays of the text mention slavery, the Middle Passage of *Fish Story* bears no discernible relation to the planned disaster that is known by that name, nor to its long and ongoing effects. No surprise, then, that the film does not address the history of the trade in abducted Africans; does not locate *that* trade as the key point in the beginning of global capital. Africa, the Caribbean, and the rest of the African diaspora are absent, the forgotten spaces of *The Forgotten Space*. And so, too, those histories and presents of slavery and colonization, of tourism, and of the establishment of military bases that containerization abets fail to appear (Llenín-Figueroa 2014, 90).[3] They are absent, that is, but for one telling exception.

The section of the film called "Mud and Sun" begins with the Port of Los Angeles / Long Beach and with the predictably failed promise post September 11, 2001, of new jobs in the Alameda Corridor. But how is one to talk of mud and sun and firmament, the Atlantic Ocean, and the United States and not take up transatlantic slavery? The crew films in a tent city that is located between two container freight lines and in the direct path of an airfreight company.[4] Sekula says that after public screenings audience members often ask him what the residents of the tent city are doing in the film. His reply is that he wanted the film to have in it the insights of those people who have been ejected from the system. Two of those ejected interviewees are middle-aged white men. Bruce R. Guthrie, who tells the film crew that they would have a hard time if they had to live in the tent city for a month, talks about not having the money to move now but says that after his mother dies and he inherits he will buy a trailer, put it on the river, and drink and fish his life away. He is identified as a former building contractor. The second white man, Robert W. Wargo, talks about the dearth of programs designed to help middle-aged men like him get a new start and about the indignity of "help" in the form of a lottery that one can only win once and that gives the winner a hotel room for three days. Wargo distinguishes himself from the other men in the tent city, whom he calls "reprobates," and he is identified in the end credits as a former mechanic. Viewers of the film are to understand that Wargo's and Guthrie's current hardship has occurred because the system has let them down.

Then there appears in front of the camera a Black woman whom we have glimpsed in the background of earlier shots.[5] She is the only Black speaking figure in the film, the only Black person who doesn't just appear in the background or in file footage. Her name is Aereile Jackson, and, in my theoretical terms, she speaks in the film from the position of the wake: from a position of deep hurt and of deep knowledge. It is painful to watch and listen to her. She is pained as she talks about her children who have been taken from her and about the cruelty of the state that cast her into this position. She talks, too, about being overweight and about her hair, and she says she wears a wig because her hair is falling out in chunks. These are symptoms of her distress. She's not mentally ill, she tells the filmmakers — she knows she is holding baby dolls in her arms, but those dolls are placeholders for her children, who were taken from her and whom she has not seen in six years. She is identified in the end credits as a "former mother" (figures 2.1, 2.2)

I had held out some hope that this film that looks at the maw of capital wouldn't simply feed her into it, wouldn't simply use her as a container for all of that unremarked-upon history, would not use her as an an asterisk or an ellipsis to move forward the narrative. I had thought that Ms. Jackson wouldn't just be a transit point ("the act or fact of passing across or through; passage or journey from one place or point to another," *Dictionary.com*). But though she provides the terms and the image, if not the exact words, that give the segment its name, Aereile Jackson appears only to be made to disappear. She is metaphor. Her appearance in the film makes no sense within the logic of the film as it unfolds; yet it makes perfect sense, for, as Stefano Harney and Fred Moten (2013, 93) write, "modernity," the very modernity that is the subject of this film, "is sutured by this hold." The *hold* is the slave ship hold; is the hold of the so-called migrant ship; is the prison; is the womb that produces blackness. When Ms. Jackson appeared in the film, she stopped time for me. In my memory, the section with her in it appeared at the end of the film and not in the first half of it. "What is time?" (Sissako 2014).

At the end of the film we get to the credits, where each of the three tent city interviewees is identified again by name and former profession: Bruce R. Guthrie is a former building contractor; Robert W. Wargo is a former mechanic; and Aereile Jackson is a "former mother."[6] In this title, "former mother," that the filmmakers tag her with there is seemingly no sense of the longue durée of that term à la partus sequitur ventrem and its afterlives. Recall her interview:

> This [and one might hear in that "this" her anticipation and condemnation of their future labeling] is like a slap in my face to me and my family. I'm not on drugs. . . . I have, these are my dolls I picked up so don't think I'm mentally ill or anything like that. I picked these up. I have a tent full of stuffed animals and dolls. This is the only thing that I have to hold on to for me to remember my children. I lost a lot and I'm homeless and I haven't seen my children since I was unable to attend court because I had no transportation. The court was way in San Bernardino and I'm way in Ontario and I lost out on my children and I haven't seen my children since and this is since 2003 and here it is 2009 so I've lost a lot. I'm trying . . . I'm hurt. I'm trying to figure out am I ever going to get the chance to be a mother again with my children I already have. I don't have my children. I'm over here in the dirt, getting darker and darker and darker. And my wig is because my hair comes out you, know, mysteriously my hair comes out, and it wasn't like that at first but I get over here and I take my hair out to wash it and stuff and it's coming out, you know. In patches. Like someone is shaving my hair off. That and I've gotten overweight to where I'm just starting to handle my weight in the hot sun and I can barely walk to the corner without getting hot and without getting hot flashes. So I'm trying to deal with my weight and my situation at the same time.[7]

Aereile Jackson has lost a lot. More than this film can or will reckon with. The violence against her is (in Wilderson's terms) not contingent, it is not violence that occurs between subjects at the level of conflict; it is gratuitous violence that occurs at the level of a structure that constitutes the Black as the constitutive outside. Put another way, the fact and the mode of the inclusion and display of Ms. Jackson's body and speech are indicative of how the film cannot understand the enactments of a language of gratuitous violence against the Black. That is, the filmmakers' language of analysis begins from the violence of her absence, and it is clear the film operates within a logic that cannot apprehend her suffering. How she is written into the film and the film's inability to comprehend her suffering are part of the orthography of the wake. The forgotten space is blackness, and as Jackson is conjured to fill it she appears as a specter. It is as if with her appearance capital is suddenly historicized in and through her body. She is opportune. They see in her an *opportunity* (from the Latin *ob-*, meaning "toward," and *portu(m)*, meaning "port").[8] But Jackson wasn't ejected from the system: she is the ejection, the abjection, by, on, through, which the system reimagines and reconstitutes itself. *"Violence precedes and exceeds blacks"* (Wilderson 2010, 76). The suffering of Black people cannot be analogized; "we" are not all claimed by life in the same way; "we" do not experience suffering on the same plain of conflict, since the Black is characterized, as Wilderson tells us, by gratuitous violence (Wilderson 2010, 126).

Sekula and Burch continue: "The cargo containers are everywhere, mobile and anonymous: 'coffins of remote labour-power,' carrying goods manufactured by invisible workers on the other side of the globe" (Sekula and Burch 2011) (figure 2.3). How are these containers that Sekula and Burch track connected with global warming and fights over water and other resources? How are they connected with the journeys that Africans make over the land, from, say, Somalia to Libya, and then across the Mediterranean Sea in an attempt to reach places like Lampedusa? How are they connected to the containerization of people prior to and during and then after that perilous sea voyage? These are questions that Sekula and Burch's film does not attempt to address.

These are the asterisked histories of slavery, of property, of thingification, and their afterlives. I can't help but see that word "risk" in "asterisk." And to link that risk and those asterisked histories to the seas and to the beginnings of the insurance trade subtended by a trade in Africans.

The history of insurance begins with the sea. Three developments are central to the conceptual framework established by marine insurance: first, the "bottomry" agreement or "sea loan" in which money is loaned at a steep rate for a voyage, the risk falling to the lender. Second, the concept of "general average," the idea that losses undertaken to save a boat (jettisoning or cutting down masts in a storm, for instance) represent a risk shared among those investing in a voyage — usually seen as the oldest form of joint-stock enterprise. And third, in the notion of "Perils of the Sea"—the earliest form of the concept of insurable risk. (Armstrong 2010, 168)

One might say that Aereile Jackson is the film's insurance—as she lends the film its vocabulary and her abjection underwrites its circulation (figure 2.4).

The risk in insurance: the asterisked human.

So I've been thinking about shippability and containerization and what is in excess of those states. What I am therefore calling the Trans*Atlantic is that s/place, condition, or process that appears alongside and in relation to the Black Atlantic but also in excess of its currents. I want to think Trans* in a variety of ways that try to get at something *about* or *toward* the range of trans*formations enacted on and by Black bodies. The asterisk after a word functions as the wildcard, and I am thinking the trans* in that way; as a means to mark the ways the slave and the Black occupy what Saidiya Hartman calls the "position of the unthought" (Hartman and Wilderson 2003). The asterisk after the prefix "trans" holds the place open for thinking (from and into that position). It speaks, as well, to a range of embodied experiences called gender and to Euro-Western gender's dismantling, its inability to hold in/on Black flesh. The asterisk speaks to a range of configurations of Black being that take the form of translation, transatlantic, transgression, transgender, transformation, transmogrification, transcontinental, transfixed, trans-Mediterranean, transubstantiation (by which process we might understand the making of bodies into flesh and then into fungible commodities while retaining the appearance of flesh and blood), transmigration, and more.

With the Trans* I am not interested in genealogy; it is not my intention to recover transgender bodies in the archive. But when Omise'eke Tinsley writes in "Black Atlantic, Queer Atlantic: Queer Imaginings of the Middle Passage" that "the Black Atlantic has always been the queer Atlantic" (Tinsley 2008, 191), we might add that the Black and queer Atlantic have always been the Trans*Atlantic. Black has always been that excess.[9] Indeed, blackness throws into crisis, whether in these

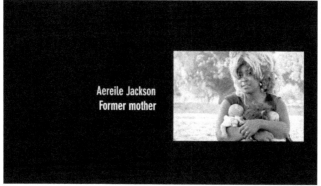

Aereile Jackson
Former mother

2.1–2.2 Stills of Aereile Jackson. 2.3 Cargo containers.
From Allan Sekula and Noël Burch, *The Forgotten Space—A Film Essay
Seeking to Understand the Contemporary Maritime World in Relation to
the Symbolic Legacy of the Sea*, 2010 (film still). Sound, color. 112 min.
Courtesy of Doc.Eye Film, Amsterdam, The Netherlands

Aereile Jackson,
Tent City
Los Angeles

Making Political Cinema –
The Forgotten Space

Darrell Varga

The making of independent cinema is always on some level a political act. Its existence is a challenge to the hegemony of the cultural industries, whether through its subject matter, its refusal to accede to prevailing social norms, or even by virtue of its regional location. It needs to be said, though, that plenty of independent media production is an audition to be let inside the culture machine. For the founding patriarch of documentary, John Grierson (the first commissioner of the NFB), art was to be used as a hammer, and he happily took on the role of propagandist from his ciné-pulpit. From Grierson we can still understand documentary as engaging the viewer not just as an individual but also as a member of society; he saw the medium as a means of fostering citizenship and enabling democracy. Documentary was important for the way that it shines a light on the technologies of power through which society is organized. The limits of the Griersonian approach, though, lie in its problem/solution structure, whereby film is used to identify issues and concerns and posit solutions for the betterment of existing society. Overall, then, we can think of political documentary as something that, broadly speaking, goes against the grain of the existing political system.

Radical political filmmaking has long been identified with movements of resistance against colonial rule and capitalist exploitation in places of underdevelopment. This kind of work is not really invested in auteurism and the art cinema tradition. Here,

2.4 Publicity still of Aereile Jackson in *Making Political Cinema*. Courtesy Jerry White and the Centre for European Studies at Dalhousie University, Halifax

places one can ever really think together, Black and (hetero)normative. That is, Black life in and out of the "New World" is always queered and more. We might say that slavery trans* all desire as it made some people into things, some into buyers, sellers, owners, fuckers, and breeders of that Black flesh. That excess is here writ large on Black bodies—as it is with the process of subjection. And it is that point, post the "rupture in the world," at which, Dionne Brand tells us, *we*, whether *we* made *that* passage or not, are "transform[ed] into being. That one door [the door of no return] transformed us into bodies emptied of being, bodies emptied of self-interpretation, into which new interpretations could be placed" (Brand 2001, 25).[10]

As we hold on to the many meanings of Trans* we can and must think and imagine laterally, across a series of relations in the ship, the hold, the wake, and the weather—in multiple Black everydays—to do what Hartman, in "Venus in Two Acts," describes as "listening for the unsaid, translating misconstrued words, and refashioning disfigured lives" and to do what NourbeSe Philip calls the necessity of "telling the story that cannot be told." "I think," Philip says, "this is what *Zong!* is attempting: to find a form to bear this story which can't be told, which must be told, but through not telling" (Saunders 2008a, 72).

To encounter people of African descent in the wake both materially and as a problem for thought is to encounter that * in the grand narrative of history; and, in the conditions of Black life and death such as those delineated by Hartman ("skewed life chances, limited access to health and education, premature death") and the ways we are positioned through and by them, the ways we occupy the "I" of Hartman's "I am the afterlife of slavery" (Hartman 2008, 6). Theorizing wake work requires a turn away from existing *disciplinary* solutions to blackness's ongoing abjection that extend the dysgraphia of the wake. It requires theorizing the multiple meanings of that abjection through inhabitation, that is, through living them in and as consciousness.

We see that dysgraphic positioning of Black people via abjection everywhere: from responses to the Black abandoned in the multiple and ongoing disasters of Hurricane Katrina to conservative *New York Times* columnist David Brooks's abhorrent January 15, 2010, op-ed on Haiti, "The Underlying Tragedy" (Brooks 2010a), in which he wrote that Haiti's problems were less a problem for "development" to solve than they were a call for a radical and radically imposed cultural shift, coming as they do as a result of "progress-resistant cultural influences."[11] Drawing from the anthology *What Works in Development?* Brooks goes on to write, "We're all supposed to politely respect each other's cultures. But some cultures are more progress-resistant than others, and a horrible tragedy was just exacerbated by one of them. . . . It's time to promote locally led paternalism. . . . to replace parts of the local culture with a highly demanding, highly intensive culture of achievement—involving everything from new child-rearing practices to stricter schools to better job performance" (Brooks 2010a). This op-ed is properly understood in the context of what *is not* said: its refusal to speak, for example, Haiti's revolutionary past and the billions of dollars in indemnity Haiti has been forced to pay to France; or the successive US military occupations and coups. Three days earlier Brooks wrote an op-ed entitled "The Tel Aviv Cluster," about the accomplishments of Jewish people all over the world. He says: "The Jewish faith encourages a belief in progress and personal accountability. Tel

Aviv has become one of the world's foremost entrepreneurial hot spots. Israel has more high-tech start-ups per capita than any other nation on earth, by far. It leads the world in civilian research-and-development spending per capita. It ranks second behind the United States in the number of companies listed on the Nasdaq. Israel, with seven million people, attracts as much venture capital as France and Germany combined" (Brooks 2010b). As with my students in Memory for Forgetting, the disaster of the Holocaust is available as human tragedy in a way that slavery, revolution, and their afterlives are not.

The asterisk is evident globally. From the death by drowning of Glenda Moore's sons Connor and Brandon (ages four and two) on Staten Island, New York in Hurricane Sandy in October 2012, to the murders of Michael Brown and Miriam Carey, to the continued crossings and drownings in the Mediterranean Sea and the Atlantic Ocean, to the policing and cordoning of Black people on and off the streets of North America, the "problem" is Black (moral) underdevelopment. The problem is blackness. The problem is blackness *is and as* underdevelopment. One can't imagine similar "culture of poverty" proclamations like Brooks's being made, for instance, in the aftermath of the devastation of the tornados in May 2013 in predominantly putatively white communities in Tornado Alley in the midwestern United States—even though many of the people living there do not or cannot take the precautions of building storm shelters, evacuating, or otherwise readying for disaster. That such things *are* said and said with such regularity about Black and blackened people is some part of what it means to be/in the wake. *"We are not only known to ourselves and to each other by that force"* (Sharpe 2012a, 828).

The Ship

THE ZONG

The sea was like slake gray of what was left of my body and the white waves . . .
I memember.
— Kamau Brathwaite, *Dream Haiti*

After spending several months off the coast of West Africa as its hold was gradually filled with abducted Africans, a slave ship named the *Zong* started its journey to Jamaica. It was originally called the *Zorgue*, and it was based in the Netherlands before being purchased in 1781 on behalf of a group of Liverpool merchants. When the *Zorgue* was captured by the British on February 10, 1781, it already had 320 abducted Africans on board; the "cargo" then was underwritten after the capture, after the ship had set sail from Cape Coast. Built to hold approximately 220 African men, women, and children; the *Zong* sailed with twice that many; there were 442 (or 470) captive Africans on board. When the ship set out for Jamaica on August 18, 1781, it had provisions for three months and the knowledge that there were a number of ports in the Caribbean where it could stop to replenish if it ran short of water and food. Records show that due to navigational errors the ship overshot Jamaica. Records show that the captain and crew reported that they decided to jettison some of the enslaved in order to "save the rest of the cargo." The transcript of *Gregson v. Gilbert* (the 1783 court case) echoes this report. It reads: "Some of the negroes died for want of sustenance, and others were thrown overboard for the preservation of the rest" (quoted in Philip 2008, 210).

The *Zong* was first brought to the awareness of the larger British public through the newspaper reports that the ship's owners (Gregson) were suing the underwriters (Gilbert) for the insurance value of those 132 (or 140 or 142) murdered Africans. Insurance claims are part of what Katherine McKittrick calls the "mathematics of black life" (McKittrick 2014), which includes that killability, that throwing overboard. "Captain Luke Collingwood thus brutally converted an uninsurable loss (general mortality) into general average loss, a sacrifice of parts of a cargo for the benefit of the whole" (Armstrong 2010, 173).

The deposed crew recounted that it was lack of water and the insurance claim that motivated that throwing overboard. They recognized that insurance monies would not be paid if those enslaved people died "a natural death." (A natural death. What would constitute a natural death here? How could their deaths *be* natural? How can the legally dead be declared murdered?) But in his testimony in court the chief mate revealed that the crew on board the *Zong* never moved to "short water," that is, at no point did they resort to water rationing (Hochschild 2006, 80). Despite the individual and combined efforts of antislavery activist Granville Sharp and the formerly enslaved antislavery activists Olaudah Equiano and Ottobah Cugoano, it would not be murder that was at issue. The events on board the *Zong* would be committed to historical memory first as the insurance claim in the case of *Gregson v. Gilbert* and only later as the murders (injury to "subjects") of 132 Africans not seen in the court to be murders. "It has been decided, whether wisely or unwisely is not now the question, that a portion of our fellow creatures may become the subject of property. This, therefore, was the throwing overboard of goods, and of part to save the residue" (quoted in Philip 2008, 211).

It may be fitting that the *Zong* most often comes to memory not as the singular ship itself but as an unnamed slaver on which the crew threw captured Africans overboard. The murderous actions of the captain and crew of that *unnamed* ship are memorialized in J. M. W. Turner's 1840 painting titled *Slave Ship: Slavers Throwing Overboard Dead and Dying—Typhon Coming On*. In the roiling, livid orpiment of Turner's painting, the dead are yoked to the dying. That Turner's slave ship lacks a proper name allows it to stand in for *every* slave ship and every slave crew, for every slave ship and all the murdered Africans in Middle Passage. As James Walvin (2011, 107) writes, "Everyone involved in the slave trade—from the grandest merchant to the roughest of deck hands—knew that there were times when the crew might have to kill the very people they had been sent to trade for and for whom they paid such high sums. Though no one would admit it openly, a crude human calculus had evolved at the heart of the slave trade and was accepted by all involved: to survive, it was sometimes necessary to kill." Turner's painting captures the horrors of the trade and refuses to collapse a singularity[12] into a ship named the *Zong*; that is, Turner's unnamed slave ship stands in for the entire enterprise, the "going concern" (Brand 2015) of the trade in captured Africans: the part for the whole. In style and content Turner's painting makes visible the questions at the center of the *Zong*—property, insurance, resistance,[13] and the question of ballast. (Think of the recent discovery of a wrecked ship off the coast of South Africa that archaeologists have determined was a slave ship because of the iron bars of ballast that they found in the wreckage. Ballast was necessary to offset the weight of the captured Africans in the hold of the ship [Cooper 2015]).

The decision of the court was achieved through an act of lexico-legal transubstantiation[14] that declared that "the case [of the *Zong*] was a simple one of maritime insurance," that is, a case of property loss and not murder. Despite the differences recorded in the numbers of Africans thrown overboard, what remains constant is that *there was that throwing overboard*; there was in fact that murder of over 130 abducted Africans. *The event*, which is to say, one version of one part of a more than four-hundred-year-long event is as follows: "29 November, at 8.00 pm, fiftyfour [*sic*] women and children were thrown overboard 'singly through the Cabin windows.' The time seems to have been chosen to coincide with the changing of the watch when the maximum number of crewmembers would be available. On 1 December a further forty-two male slaves were thrown overboard from the quarterdeck" (Lewis 2007, 364). We read that "the next day it rained, and the crew collected enough fresh drinking water to add a three weeks supply to the ship's store" (Vincent Brown 2008, 159). Nevertheless, counter to the logic that lack of water is what motivated these acts that would circumvent the insurance rules of "natural death," "in the course of the next days thirty-six more slaves were thrown overboard and a further ten jumped into the water by themselves. Kelsall later considered that 'the outside number of drowned amounted to 142 in the whole'" (Lewis 2007, 364).

When the *Zong* finally arrived on the Black River in Jamaica on December 22, 1781, there were 208 living Africans on board. When the Jamaican *Cornwall Chronicle* listed those Africans for sale, they noted that "'the vessel . . . was in great distress' having jettisoned some 130 slaves" (Lewis 2007, 364). With that notation of great distress, the paper did not (mean to) gesture toward the enslaved. They did not (mean to) account for the psychic and material toll the long journey of forced abduction, want, and incredible violence had taken on the enslaved (violence not marked as violence nor abduction nor want). It was the ship that was in great distress, not the enslaved. Here, if not everywhere, as we will see, the ship is distinct from the slave. When the sale took place on January 9, 1782, the remaining enslaved people sold for an average of thirty-six pounds each—above the thirty-pound price at which they were insured. But, of course those enslaved *people* were also in great physical and psychic distress; witnesses to and survivors of the extravagant violences of the ship, its living death, and mass murder. Perhaps, especially, that one enslaved man who, thrown overboard, managed to climb back onto the ship.

How does one account for surviving the ship when the ship and the un/survival repeat?

ZONG!

We sing for death, we sing for birth. That's what we do. We sing.
— Patricia Saunders, "Defending the Dead, Confronting the Archive"

What does it look like, entail, and mean to attend to, care for, comfort, and defend, those already dead, those dying, and those living lives consigned to the possibility of always-imminent death, life lived in the presence of death; to live this imminence and immanence as and in the "wake"? I turn here to NourbeSe Philip's *Zong!*. Each of the numbered poems in "Os," *Zong's!* first section, is composed of words taken from the court case of *Gregson v. Gilbert*. Below the line of the poems in "Os" appear Philip's annotations—names for those Africans on board the *Zong* who had no names that their captors were bound to recognize or record.[15] Those now-named Africans in "Os" (Os as ordinary seaman, mouth, opening, or bone) are the bones of the text of *Zong!*

Zong!, Philip says, "is hauntological; it is a work of haunting, a wake of sorts, where the spectres of the undead make themselves present" (Philip 2008, 201). The dead appear in Philip's *Zong!*, beyond the logic of the ledger, beyond the mathematics of insurance, and it is they who underwrite the poems that comprise "Os." Philip aspirates those submerged lives and brings them back to the text from which they were ejected. Likewise, in the structure of *Zong!* the number of names of those people underwriting the enterprise of slavery do not match the number of the thrown and jumped, and so, with that too, Philip dispenses with a particular kind of fidelity to the invention of the historical archive.

"*Zong!* #15" begins with the statement/imperative/injunction to "defend the dead." I reproduce it here. Philip provides names.

"What is the word for bringing bodies back from water? From a 'liquid grave'?" (Philip 2008, 201). The word that Philip arrives at is *exaqua*. But there is no retrieving bone from its watery wake. There is no bringing the bodies from the *Zong* and so many other past and present ships up from the water or back to the shore. There are, as Philip knows, no bones to recover.

Zong! #15

    defend the dead

              weight of circumstance

    ground

        to usual &

            etc

        where the ratio of just

    in less than

          is necessary

              to murder

    the subject in property

    the save in underwriter

              where etc tunes justice

              and the *ratio* of murder

              is

              the usual in occurred

        Akilah Falope Ouma Weke Jubade

          the just in ration

          the suffer in loss

               defend the dead

               the weight

                        in

circumstance

        ached in necessary

               the ration in just

        age the act in the *ave* to justice

        Micere Ndale Omowunmi Ramla Ajani

A ship moving through water generates a particular pattern of waves; the bow wave is in front of the ship, and that wave then spreads out in the recognizable V pattern on either side of and then behind the ship. The size of the bow wave dictates how far out the wake starts. Waves that occur in the wake of the ship move at the same speed as the ship. From at least the sixteenth century onward, a major part of the ocean engineering of ships has been to minimize the bow wave and therefore to minimize the wake. But the effect of trauma is the opposite. It is to make maximal the wake. The transverse waves are those waves that run through the back; they are perpendicular to the direction of the motion of the ship. Transverse waves look straight but are actually arcs of a circle. And every time, every instant that the boat is moving through water it has the potential to generate a new wave.[16]

Certainly the *Zong*, far away from any landmass, would have been in deep water, and any object, or person thrown overboard would have been in deepwater waves. Once in the water that thrown overboard person would have experienced the circular or bobbing motion of the wake and would have been carried by that wake for at least for a short period of time. It is likely, though, that because many of those enslaved people were sick and were likely emaciated or close to it, they would have had very little body fat; their bodies would have been denser than seawater. It is likely, then, that those Africans, thrown overboard, would have floated just a short while, and only because of the shapes of their bodies. It is likely, too, that they would have sunk relatively quickly and drowned relatively quickly as well. And then there were the sharks that always traveled in the wake of slave ships.

There have been studies done on whales that have died and have sunk to the seafloor. These studies show that within a few days the whales' bodies are picked almost clean by benthic organisms — those organisms that live on the seafloor. My colleague Anne Gardulski tells me it is most likely that a human body would not make it to the seafloor intact. What happened to the bodies? By which I mean, what happened to the components of their bodies in salt water? Anne Gardulski tells me that because nutrients cycle through the ocean (the process of organisms eating organisms is the cycling of nutrients through the ocean), the atoms of those people who were thrown overboard are out there in the ocean even today. They were eaten, organisms processed them, and those organisms were in turn eaten and processed, and the cycle continues. Around 90 to 95 percent of the tissues of things that are eaten in the water column get recycled. As Anne told me, "Nobody dies of old age in the ocean."

The amount of time it takes for a substance to enter the ocean and then leave the ocean is called residence time. Human blood is salty, and sodium, Gardulski tells me, has a residence time of 260 million years. And what happens to the energy that is produced in the waters? It continues cycling like atoms in residence time. We, Black people, exist in the residence time of the wake, a time in which "everything is now. It is all now" (Morrison 1987, 198).

> *The sea was like slake gray of what was left of my body and the white waves. . . . I memember.*

HOW A GIRL BECOMES A SHIP

First another epigraph from *Dream Haiti* by Kamau Brathwaite and then a long quotation from June Jordan's "The Difficult Miracle of Black Poetry in America or Something like a Sonnet for Phillis Wheatley."

Brathwaite: "I do not know why I am here—how I came to be on board this ship, this navel of my ark."

Now Jordan:

> It was not natural. And she was the first. Come from a country of many tongues tortured by rupture, by theft, by travel like mismatched clothing packed down into the cargo hold of evil ships sailing, irreversible, into slavery. Come to a country to be docile and dumb, to be big and breeding, easily, to be turkey/horse/cow, to be cook/carpenter/plow, to be 5'6" 140 lbs., in good condition and answering to the name of Tom or Mary: to be bed bait: to be legally spread legs for rape by the master/the master's son/the master's overseer/the master's visiting nephew: to be nothing human nothing family nothing from nowhere nothing that screams nothing that weeps nothing that dreams nothing that keeps anything/anyone deep in your heart: to live forcibly illiterate, forcibly itinerant: to live eyes lowered head bowed: to be worked without rest, to be worked without pay, to be worked without thanks, to be worked day up to nightfall: to be three-fifths of a human being

at best: to be this valuable/this hated thing among strangers who purchased your life and then cursed it unceasingly: to be a slave: to be a slave. Come to this country a slave and how should you sing?

. . .

How should there be Black poets in America? It was not natural. And she was the first. It was 1761—so far back before the revolution that produced these United States, so far back before the concept of freedom disturbed the insolent crimes of this continent—in 1761, when seven year old Phillis stood, as she must, when she stood nearly naked, as small as a seven year old, by herself, standing on land at last, at last after the long, annihilating horrors of the Middle Passage. Phillis, standing on the auctioneer's rude platform: Phillis For Sale.

Was it a nice day?

Does it matter?

Should she muse on the sky or remember the sea? Until then Phillis had been somebody's child. Now she was about to become somebody's slave.

. . .

When the Wheatleys arrived at the auction they greeted their neighbors, they enjoyed this business of mingling with other townsfolk politely shifting about the platform, politely adjusting positions for gain of a better view of the bodies for sale. The Wheatleys were good people. They were kind people. They were openminded and thoughtful. They looked at the bodies for sale. They looked and they looked. This one could be useful for that. That one might be useful for this. But then they looked at that child, that Black child standing nearly naked, by herself. Seven or eight years old, at the most, and frail. Now that was a different proposal! Not a strong body, not a grown set of shoulders, not a promising wide set of hips, but a little body, a delicate body, a young, surely terrified face! John Wheatley agreed to the whim of his wife, Suzannah. He put in his bid. He put down his cash. He called out the numbers. He competed successfully. He had a good time. He got what he wanted. He purchased yet another slave. He bought that Black girl standing on the platform, nearly naked. He gave this new slave to his wife and Suzannah Wheatley was delighted. She and her husband went home. They rode there by carriage. They took that new slave with them. An old slave commanded the horses that pulled the carriage that carried the Wheatleys home, along with the new slave, that little girl they named Phillis.

Why did they give her that name? (Jordan 2003, 174–76)

We know that the Wheatleys name that African girl child Phillis after the slave ship (the *Phillis*) on which her transatlantic abduction through the Middle Passage was completed. The Wheatleys made an experiment of her. They allowed and encouraged this Phillis, child of a "bitterly anonymous man and a woman," to "develop," to become literate, to write poetry, to become "the first Black human being to be published in America" (Jordan 2003, 176).[17]

Ninety years after "Phillis Miracle" (Jordan 2003, 176), Louis Agassiz, one of the founders of the American school of ethnology, commissioned daguerreotypes of seven enslaved men and women, among them two sets of Africa-born fathers and their US-born daughters, all meant to be "pure," unmiscegenated examples of the race. We know that the daguerreotypes of Renty (Congo) and Jack (Guinea), the Africa-born men, and the "country-born" daughters Delia and Drana are meant to reveal what blackness looks like and how to look at blackness. They are meant to make visible separate development and separate species. "Agassiz's hope [was] to enlist the aid of photography so as to prove his claims that not all humans are of the same species and that the black race is inferior to the white one, alongside the transformation of these photographed people into illustrations for a scientific claim" (Azoulay 2008, 166). Put another way, the daguerreotypes of the fathers and daughters are meant to make visible the ship, *and* its wake, *in the slave*. Given that the law of slavery was partus sequitur ventrem, one might ask why it is fathers and daughters who are photographed here and not fathers and sons, mothers and sons, or the mothers (through whom slavery legally passes) and the daughters through whom, if they give birth, it will also pass? What might the subject choice of these daguerreotypes tell us about the photographic framings and subjections of racialsexualgender and of Black resisting objects? What might it tell us about how this particular framing will reach into and across the present and future—to arrest *and* set in motion how all Black images will be seen in their wake? In the movement in the United States from slave law to black codes, to Jim Crow, to what will come after, this projection into the future is an attempt to submit Black inheritance to a patriarchal order that will then be seen to fail to *take hold* after the date of formal emancipation, thereby marking *blackness* as pathology through to future generations.[18] Despite all its transformative power, blackness, here, will be seen to fail to be transformed. Put another way, in and out of the United States this ethnographic gaze will be put into practice across time and administrative process, and the injury will then be seen to slip from the conditions of slavery, colonialism, segregation, lynching, touristic display, ethnographic display, incarceration, vigilantism, gentrification, "immigrant camps and detention centers," and state murder, to social and other "scientific claims" about blackness, about Black being, itself.

I was struck on first seeing those daguerreotypes of Jack, Delia, Renty, and Drana, as I was by my encounter with a photograph taken 160 years later that I found when I entered the archives of photographs of disaster in the aftermath of the catastrophic earthquake that hit Haiti on January 12, 2010. These photographs echoed the photographs of that disaster, and disastrous response to, Hurricane Katrina on the US Gulf Coast in 2005. It was not the first time I had cautiously entered this archive, but this time I was stopped by this photograph of a Haitian girl child, ten years old at the most (figure 2.5). A third of the image, the left-hand side, is blurry, but her face is clear; it's what is in focus. She is alive. Her eyes are open. She is lying on a black stretcher; her head is on a cold pack, there is an uncovered wound over and under her right eye and a piece of paper stuck to her bottom lip, and she is wearing what seems to be a hospital gown. She is looking at or past the camera; her look reaches out to me. Affixed to her forehead is a piece of transparent tape with the word *Ship* written on it.

Who put it there? Does it matter?

What is the look in her eyes? What do I do with it?

When I stumbled upon *that* image of *this* girl child with the word *Ship* taped to her forehead, it was the look in her eyes that first stopped me, and then, with its coming into focus, that word *Ship* threatened to obliterate every and anything else I could see. (What was it doing there?) But I returned to her face; what was the look in her eyes? And what was I being called to by and with her look at me and mine at her? Over the years I have returned repeatedly to this image to try to account for what I saw there or thought I might see. Where is she looking? Who and what is she looking for? Who can look back? Does she know that there is a piece of tape on her forehead? Does she know what that piece of tape says? Does she know that she is destined for a ship? Her eyes look back at me, like Delia's eyes, like Drana's. I marked her youth, the scar on the bridge of her nose that seems to continue through one eyebrow, her eyes and eyelashes, the uncovered wounds, a bit of paper, and a leaf. In this photographic arrangement I see her and I feel with and for her as she is disarranged by this process. I see this intrusion into her life and world at the very moment it is, perhaps not for the first time, falling apart. In her I recognize myself, by which I mean, I recognize the common conditions of Black being in the wake.

Where was her mother? Her father? Whom did she turn to when scared? (Saunders 2008a, 77)

Twenty years after Phillis, the ship and the girl, arrive in Boston, Massachusetts, the *Zong* achieves notoriety through the binding and throwing overboard of 132 (or 140 or 142) Africans in order to collect insurance.[19] The text of the 1783 court case *Gregson v. Gilbert* tells us that this was not a case of murder, tells us that "it has been decided, whether wisely or unwisely is not now the question, that a portion of our fellow creatures may become property. This, therefore, was a throwing overboard of goods, and of part to save the residue" (quoted in Philip 2008, 211). Originally named the *Zorg* (or *Zorgue*), which translates from the Dutch into English as "care," the ship becomes the *Zong* after it was captured in war and bought by a Liverpool slave company and an error was made in the repainting of the name. We should pause for at least a moment on the *fact* of a slave ship named *Care* (care registering, here, as "the provision of what is necessary for the health, welfare, maintenance, and protection of someone or something," as support and protection but also as grief) *before, and as*, we attempt to understand that

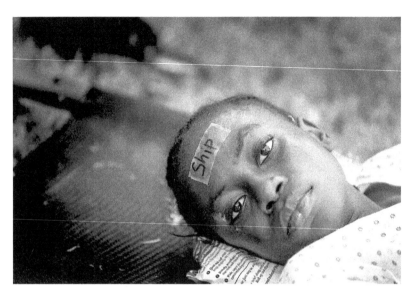

2.5 Haiti struggles for aid and survival after earthquake.
© Joe Raedle / Getty Images

single word *Ship* attached to that small Black female body in the after-math of the Haitian earthquake in 2010. Is *Ship* a proper name? A destination? An imperative? A signifier of the im/possibility of Black life under the conditions of what, Stephanie Smallwood tells us, "would become an enduring project in the modern Western world [of] probing the limits up to which it is possible to discipline the body without extinguishing the life within" (Smallwood 2008, 35–36)? Is *Ship* a reminder and/or remainder of the Middle Passage, of the difference between life and death? Of those other Haitians in crisis sometimes called boat people? Or is *Ship* a reminder and/or remainder of the ongoing migrant and refugee crises unfolding in the Mediterranean Sea and the Indian and Atlantic Oceans? Given how visual and literary culture evoke and invoke the Middle Passage with such deliberate and reflexive dysgraphic unseeing, I cannot help but extrapolate.

Compare that image to the 1992 photograph of another Haitian girl child (figure 2.6). She is also seven or eight years old, ten at most, and she is holding a ship. That photograph is taken during the height of the forced exodus of Haitian refugees—those people adrift, sometimes picked up and incarcerated, and other times, most often, turned back by the US Coast Guard and other nations. As Kaiama Glover (2011) reminds us, the "ship" indexes the "floating detention centers controlled by government agencies of the United States and the United Kingdom . . . where 'ghost prisoners'—individuals denied protective anchoring to a sovereign homeland—languish in the international waters of the Indian Ocean. . . . [as well as those] 20th and 21st century Haitians . . . shipwrecked and lost at sea or turned away from hostile beaches in Jamaica, the Bahamas, Florida . . ." We know, too, that "the United States has intercepted thousands of Haitian refugees at sea and forcibly returned them" (DeLoughrey 2010, 708). The Haitian girl child in this photograph stands in front of a desk and before a man and a woman seated behind and to the side of the desk. Their backs are to the camera. They are taking down her information, checking boxes, in a ledger of some sort. The woman is wearing gold earrings; there appears to be an epaulet on the shoulder of the man's shirt. The little girl stands in front of them, in front of the desk on which a model ship rests (a model Coast Guard cutter?), and her hands are on the ship. No one appears to be with her there. Her face is serious, her look concentrated. *What is the look in her eyes? What do I do with it?* "*Where was her mother? Her father? Whom did she turn to when scared?*" The ledger that renders us illegible as human returns and repeats, as does the ship. In the 1992 photograph we see a ship and we see a little girl; we see a little girl holding a ship and know that a ship will hold this girl, precariously. The photograph is captioned "Haitian Boat People" and the accompanying description reads: "A small child waits while her personal information is written down in preparation for the voyage from Haiti to the United States. US President Bill Clinton offered temporary asylum to fleeing Haitians who have abandoned the poverty and corruption of their homeland. Thousands of refugees head for the shores of Florida, attempting the 500 kilometer journey in rickety boats made from their former homes." The phrase *boat people*, applied to those Haitians leaving the country under force, *reflects*, enacts, and attempts to erase its particular and brutal violences, and this ship and this girl enact a prior and ongoing instance of eponymity.[20] "*A boat, even a wrecked and wretched boat still has all the possibilities of moving*" (Brand 2002, 92).

Of course, after the initial obliterating shock of seeing the 2010 photograph, one searches for clues to help understand, perhaps explain, the violence of someone placing the word *Ship* on the forehead of

2.6 Haitian boat people. © Jacques Langevin/Sygma/Corbis

a young Black girl. One pulls back so that the other details I described become visible: the gown, the leaf, those big brown eyes with their impossibly long eyelashes and an uncovered wound under the right one, the stretcher and the cold pack. In addition to indexing all that Glover cautions us to keep in mind, we might allow that the label *Ship* is expedient, that the people who put it there are trying to help, that it's a signifier of medical necessity in the midst of disaster and the disorder that follows. Someone wanted to mark this girl child for evacuation, wanted to make sure she got on that ship. But an allowance for intention aside, one of the larger questions that arises from the image is how does one mark someone *for* a space—the ship—who is already marked *by it*?

In *Beloved* (Morrison 1987, 61), Sethe asks her mother, "Mark me, too. Mark the mark on me too" (the mark being the brand under her breast that she shows Sethe so that her daughter might identify her if her face is destroyed in the event that their revolt is unsuccessful). The mark was burned into Sethe's mother's flesh on the littoral before she was stowed in the hold of the ship. But it is also more than that. It is a mark consistent with the branding that would turn those Africans into property and with a Kongo cosmogram that marks the bearer of it as an initiate. In the latter case, it connects the living and the dead, and it signifies that the bearer "understands the meaning of life as a process shared with the dead below the river or the sea" (Stuckey 1992, 103; see also Thompson 1984). The mark in *Beloved* is connected to the ship on which Sethe's mother is forced to cross into slavery and to what was before and what comes in its wake. The mother's response to Sethe's request that she "mark the mark on me too" is a slap because she knows what that mark means and she knows, and Sethe will come to know, that she is already marked. The mother also knows that to live in the wake, Sethe will have to remake the meaning of the mark, as she too will come to "understand the meaning of life as a process shared with the dead below the river or the sea" (Bolster 1998, 65). We must ask, again, with Spillers (2003b, 207), whether "this phenomenon of marking and branding actually 'transfers' from one generation to another, finding its various symbolic substitutions in an efficacy of meanings that repeat the initiating moments."

To return to the image of the little girl with the word *Ship* on her forehead, it also strikes me that of the forty-two photographs in the online image gallery of the aftermath of the 2010 earthquake where I first found this one, this is the only one in which the caption does not label the person photographed as male or female, boy or girl.[21] And this seems to me to be significant in a culture so intent on that marking.[22] When I look at this photograph I see a young girl, to quote Jordan on Phillis Wheatley, "a delicate body, a young, surely terrified face" (Jordan 2003, 176)! And I wonder if it is the word *Ship* that has confused the photographer and the caption writers. A synchronicity (a singularity) of thought emerges here. And it occurs to me that the person who affixed that word *Ship* to her forehead emerges as another kind of underwriter, here, whose naming operates within the logics and arithmetics that would also render her a meager child, as in one who occupies less space in the hold of a ship (figure 2.7).

To be clear, the optic that registers this girl only as "child" is one that indexes at least a certain inability to see, but what is at stake here is not a correction of that vision, not an expansion of that category of "girl" to include this child. Rather, what I am indexing here arrives by way of Spillers's "Mama's Baby, Papa's Maybe" (2003b, 208), that "our task [is to make] a place for this different social subject." We should remember not only that the "death rate on the trans-Atlantic voyage to the New World was staggeringly high" but also that slave ships "were more than floating tombs. They were floating laboratories, offering researchers a chance to examine the course of diseases in fairly controlled, quarantined environments. Doctors and medical researchers could take advantage of high mortality rates to identify a bewildering number of symptoms, classify them into diseases and hypothesize about their causes" (Glover 2011). We should remember, too, those in the present, seen and still abandoned at sea—like those on board what has come to be called "the left-to-die boat."[23] And remembering this, we should pause, again, on the name and provenance of the ship that that little girl is destined for—a US *military medical ship* named *Comfort*. "US," "military," "comfort," and "allopathic medicine"—each and together being terms whose connection in the lives and on the bodies of Black people everywhere and anywhere on the globe—warrant at least a deep suspicion if not outright alarm: from those experiments on board the floating laboratory of the slave (and migrant) ship, to J. Marion Sims's surgical experiments conducted without anesthesia on enslaved women; to the outbreaks of cholera in Haiti introduced by UN troops; to experiments with mustard gas on US Black soldiers in World War II to produce an "ideal chemical soldier"; to the Tuskegee and Guatemala syphilis experiments and their ripple effects; to the dubious origins and responses to the crisis of Ebola; to the ongoing practice of forced sterilization; to recent studies that show again and again that Black people in the United States receive inferior health care because they are believed to feel less pain.[24] We might pause, too, because that ship named *Comfort* is too close in name to another one originally named *Care*, the *Zorgue* renamed the *Zong*. But in this particular 2010 un-naming, in this marking of a quantity known only as "child," we glimpse that *oceanic ungendering* that Spillers theorized in "Mama's Baby, Papa's Maybe" (2003b, 214) as "those African persons in 'Middle Passage' . . . literally suspended in the oceanic, if we think of the latter . . . as an analogy on undifferentiated identity." We continue with Spillers (2003a, 206), "Under these conditions we lose at least *gender* difference *in the outcome*, and the female body and the male body become a territory of cultural and political maneuver, not at all gender-related, gender-specific."

The question for theory is how to live in the wake of slavery, in slavery's afterlives, the afterlife of property, how, in short, to inhabit and rupture this episteme with their, with our, knowable lives. "What else is there to know" now? In excess of: "Hers is the same fate of every other Black Venus" (Hartman 2008, 2)?

I didn't want to leave her (this girl child with the word *Ship* affixed to her forehead) as I found her in an archive of hurt and death and destruction that reveals neither her name nor her sex nor any other details of her life. One AP caption tells us: "An injured child waits to be flown for treatment on the USNS *Comfort*."[25] The second AP caption reads, "Port-Au-Prince, Haiti—January 21: A child waits to be medevaced by US Army soldiers from the 82nd Airborne to the USNS Comfort on January 21, 2010 in Port-au-Prince, Haiti. Planeloads of rescuers and relief supplies headed to Haiti as governments and aid agencies launched a massive relief operation after a powerful earthquake that may have killed thousands. Many buildings were reduced to rubble by the 7.0-strong quake on January 12."[26] But a *"voice interrupts: says she"* (McKittrick 2014, 17).

And so this Girl from the archives of disaster of the first month of the second decade of the twenty-first century is evocative of another two girls on board that slave ship *Recovery* in the midst of the long disaster of Atlantic slavery whose effects are still unfolding and whose stories Hartman tells by untelling in "Venus in Two Acts." And they are evocative of other contemporary girls, as they, too, are mis/seen and all too often un/accounted for.

A meager story is not a failure. *"We are not only known to ourselves and to each other through and by that force"* (Sharpe 2012a, 828). And I was not drawn to this young girl's image to enact more violence. If I could help it, I did not want to resubject her in those ways. Echoing the poet Claire Harris (1984, 38) in "Policeman Cleared in Jaywalking Case," I think, "Look you, child, I signify . . . the child was black and female . . . and therefore mine, Listen." What happens when we look at and listen to these and other Black girls across time? What is made in our encounters with them? This looking makes ethical demands on the viewer; demands to imagine otherwise; to reckon with the fact that the archive, too, is invention. Harris's poem takes its title from a news item that appeared in the *Edmonton Journal* in 1983. The girl is fifteen and Black and she is stopped by the police for jaywalking. She is "terrified" (a bystander recalls) and unable to produce identification with a photo on it that will satisfy their gaze, their rules, and so she is arrested, "stripped/spread/searched" (Harris 1984, 36). The second girl in the poem is the poet, who at fifteen is daydreaming when she steps, thoughtless, into a busy street in Trinidad. "I was released with a smile/with sympathy sent on in the warm green morning/Twenty years later to lift a newspaper and see my fifteen year old self/still dumb/now in a police car/still shivering as the morning rolls past but here/sick in the face of such vicious intent" (Harris 1984, 36). In the face of the Canadian state's "vicious intent" Harris is moved to imagine across time and space to retrieve the incident from her childhood in order to place it alongside the contemporary one, and to speak and write to and from an imagined and lived otherwise. So when Hartman in "Venus in Two Acts" concludes: "So it was better to leave them as I had found them" and then two pages later asks, "In the end, was it better to leave them as I found them?" the statement and the question perform an epanalepsis: "the repetition of a word or words after an intervening word or words, whether for emphasis or clarity, as to resume a construction after a lengthy parenthesis"; a "liaison between words and sentences."[27] Between the statement and the interrogative is the interregnum; and in that interval the "something—anything—else" can and does appear.

In the 2010 photograph of a Haitian girl child marked with *Ship*, we lose whatever attempt at a first name Phillis granted Phillis Wheatley, lose something like gender and individuation. *"Yet a voice interrupts: says she"* (McKittrick 2014, 17). Recall that in the archives Spillers, Philip, Hartman, and others most often encounter not individuals, but columns in which subjects have been transformed into cargo marked in the ledger with the notation "negro man, ditto, negro woman, ditto." "There were," on the *Zong*'s and other ships' manifestos, Philip tells us, "no names—the lists of slaves in the book were simply identified as 'Negro man' or 'Negro woman' at the top of the ledger and the account book followed by 'ditto' all down the page, with the exception of one gloss, 'meagre,' allowed with reference to 'negro girl'—'negro girl meagre.'" She continues, "And just in that one word . . . I halted when I saw the word, and I thought, there is a whole story in that word, 'meagre'" (Saunders 2008a, 77).

Phillis Wheatley, daughter of a "bitterly anonymous man and a woman" (Jordan 2003, 176), was "meager" (a meager, sickly child according to some accounts), never really a girl; at least not "girl" in any way that operates as a meaningful signifier in Euro-Western cultures; no such persons recognizable as "girl" being inspected, sold, and purchased at auction in the "New World." Likewise, to some, Phillis was never really a poet. Most famously not to Thomas Jefferson, who wrote in Query XIV of *Notes on the State of Virginia* ([1785] 1998, 147), "Misery is often the parent of the most affecting touches in poetry.—Among the blacks is misery, God knows, but no poetry..... Religion indeed has produced a Phyllis Whately; but it could not produce a poet. The compositions published under her name are below the dignity of criticism."

In that 2010 photo the meager child is not Phillis, but *Ship*; that is, she is not a *particular* ship/girl named Phillis but *any* ship/child/girl; the part for the whole. And, while this is the only photograph like this that I have found, my experience of photographs of disasters that happen in Black spaces and to Black people is that they usually feature groups of Black people, to quote Elizabeth Alexander, in "pain for public consumption" (Alexander 1995, 92) whether those Black people are in Los Angeles, New Orleans, Sierra Leone, the Dominican Republic, Lampedusa, Liberia, or Haiti (figures 2.9–2.13).

Philip in *Zong!* and Fred D'Augiar in *Feeding the Ghosts* tell us that there were on board that slave ship *Zong many* meager girls. So, on the one hand, we can imagine this photographer pulling back the shot to reveal not one Black girl child but row after row after row of Black girls, boys, men, and women with the word *Ship* affixed to their foreheads. Alternatively, given the ways Black suffering forms the backdrop against which another kind of "human drama" (capital H) is staged, we might also realize that pulling back the shot may reveal that she is the only one so labeled for evacuation. Marked as the *Ship*/the child (like The Phillis); saved (?) in order to be subjected yet again, because we are only usually singular, only the one, in an extraordinariness that, from one point of view obscures suffering in order to produce a "miracle Phillis," and rarely "singular" or "one" in our putatively visible suffering or vulnerability despite that being, for some, all that there is to be seen. It was not better to leave her as I found her. In my reading and praxis of wake work, I have tried to position myself with her, in the wake.

October 3, 2013. A ship filled with 500 African migrants caught fire, capsized, and sank one half-mile off the coast of the Italian island of Lampedusa. Like the *Zong*, which was built to carry at most 200 people but was packed with over 440 captive Africans, this unnamed ship was

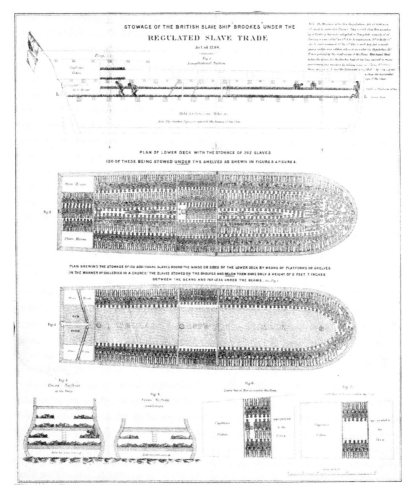

2.7 Stowage of the British slave ship *Brookes* under the regulated slave trade act of 1788, ca. 1788. Etching. Library of Congress Rare Book and Special Collections Division. LC- LC-USZ62–34160

meant to hold fewer than half the number of people on it. Over 300 of the men, women, and children on board were killed. "Deep sea divers 'unpacked a wall of people' from the hull of a smuggler's trawler on the seafloor near this Italian island on Monday, gingerly untangling the dead would-be migrants in the latest and most painstaking phase of a recovery operation following the ship's fiery capsizing,"[28] a staggering loss of life and a "human cargo" that, we learn for the smugglers was "worth almost €500,000." Two hundred thirty years after the crew on board the slave ship *Zong* threw overboard those living Africans, that word *cargo* repeats, and so do the horrors of the holding, the throwing, and the beating. African migrants are exposed "to inhuman levels of violence," stabbed and thrown overboard, shot and thrown overboard, migrants shut in the "dark and suffocating hold," while others are packed on deck—standing on the door to the hold; the perils are not now, and never have been, evenly distributed. As newspapers report on these present disasters and the migrants' states of distress, are we to imagine that some kind of repair is done with the contemporary newspapers recognition of their physical and psychic distress and the addition of the adjective *human* to the noun *cargo*? The addition of the word *human* to *cargo* does nothing, here, to ameliorate the ghosting these ships do of transatlantic slavery or the afterlives of slavery or the afterlives of property. *"Pastness . . . is a position. Thus, in no way can we identify the past as past"* (Trouillot 1997, 15).

Survivors of that October 2013 shipwreck report that the smuggler set a fire to attract the attention of the fishermen in the waters and the authorities on shore; they report that maritime authorities had the vessel under surveillance but did not come to the struggling and then burning ship's aid. They report that the fire quickly got out of control and that more than twenty minutes elapsed before any help came. "Local yachters" said "that they thought they were hearing a gaggle of seagulls, rather than human beings on the precipice of death. . . . The refusal to believe and to know, or more so, the desire to misrecognize black suffering, naturalized as so much wildlife" (Saucier and Woods 2014, 18).

"These bodies are all speaking," she [Mayor Giusi Nicolini] told the BBC, of the corpses in lacquered green and blue body bags. If that's true, it's a troubling sort of ventriloquism. What if next time, such voices weren't invited to the table only as corpses—if their complexities were heard, say, before their callings-out could be taken for the cries of seagulls? (Stillman 2013)

Hearing high-pitched cries, they looked out to sea to find that the source of the noise wasn't birds (as they'd first assumed) but Eritrean migrants shouting for help, their bodies thrashing. A large portion were women and children fleeing conflict and poverty by way of Libya, only to be hastily drowning, within eyesight of the Italian shoreline, in the same waters they'd hoped would rescript their lives. (Stillman 2013)

"For five hours we were floating, using the dead bodies of our companions," a survivor named Germani Nagassi, age thirty, told CNN this week. "There is nothing worse than this. There were many children. There was a mother with her four children, a mother with an infant, all lost at sea. My mind is scarred and in a terrible condition." (Chance 2013)

"Rescuers and local fishermen described the scene as a 'sea of heads' with scores of people waving arms and screaming for help in the water." From the fishermen we learn that many of them did not go to the aid of the drowning passengers because to do so would be to risk having their boats seized under Italian law. Says one fisherman, "This immigration law is killing people"; while another reports, the "coastguards stopped him saving more people" and "that rescue workers refused to take people from his full boat so he could rescue more, because it was against their protocol."[29]

The details accumulate like the ditto ditto in the archives.

Rescuers describe their "shock" when they find among the hundreds of the dead a woman, aged approximately twenty, with a newborn baby boy still connected to her by an umbilical cord. They report losing their detachment. They say, "We could not have gone back up without trying to do something for her. . . . We took her out of the boat forming a human chain with our arms. Then we laid her on the seabed. We tied her with a rope to other bodies and then . . . we rose with them from the depths of the sea to the light." (Davies 2013)

We stumble upon her in exorbitant circumstances that yield no picture of the everyday life, no pathway to her thoughts, no glimpse of the vulnerability of her face or of what looking at such a face might demand. (Hartman 2008, 2)

The Italian rescuers' feeling, though, will not mitigate that this young woman's care will be transformed into her incapacity to mother (à la partus sequitur ventrem) and that so-called incapacity will come to stand in for *their* crimes (of imperialism, colonialism, privatization, mineral and resource extraction, environmental destruction, etc.). The rescuers' sympathy does not mitigate Fortress Europe's death-dealing policies. Hartman and Wilderson (2003, 189–90) remind us of this: "There's a structural prohibition (rather than merely a willful refusal) against whites being the allies of blacks due to this . . . 'species' division between what it means to be a subject and what it means to be an object: a structural antagonism."

The sea is history. (Derek Walcott quoted in Brand 2001, 12)

These scenes return us to Brathwaite's *Dream Haiti* and its depiction of a "collapse of the space and time separating the contemporary interdiction of Haitian refugees at sea and the long history of patrolling African bodies in the Middle Passage" (DeLoughrey 2010, 708). The energies of the wake pattern force us back to Brathwaite's epigraph, with which this section began—*"I do not know why I am here, how I came to be on board this ship, this navel of my ark"*—with its homophones of *naval* with two *a*'s, as in maritime or aquatic forces, as in navies or warships, and *navel* with an *e*, as in the remainder of the umbilicus; the *ark* with a *k*, as it gestures to Noah's saving ship, to the curse upon Canaan, and also the *arc* with a *c*, as it references routes traveled, circumference, and the transverse waves of the wake.

It is those who survive this ordeal, repeated multiple times a week—not the multinational corporations and governments that compel the ordeal—who face criminal investigation, further containment, and repatriation.

If the crime is blackness, is the sentence the circuit between ship and shore? A girl named after a ship. A girl with the word *Ship* on her forehead. A girl holding a ship. A girl whose school is a "ship in the storm."[30] The wrecked and wretched boats keep moving. *The details accumulate like the ditto ditto in the archives; "we don't even know [all of] their names."*

THE BLACK MEDITERRANEAN

a boat, even a wrecked and wretched boat still has all the possibilities of moving
— Dionne Brand, *Inventory*

The Mediterranean has a long history in relation to slavery. "What we are facing today is a new declination of an old and repressed issue that haunts and composes the European project and modernity itself: the 'black Mediterranean' is a constituent unit od analysis for understanding contemporary forms of policing Europe's borders."[31]

"How did you travel like this? This is a fiberglass boat, and you have this small child, and your whole boat is broken, and you have this small child, and your whole boat is broken." . . ."How did you get here? Only by the grace of God . . ." "When they saw the boat, everybody said, 'It's not possible with this boat, it's a complete wreck.'" (Venice Biennale)

The evening of March 26, 2011, late, seventy-two African women, men, and children left Tripoli in a crowded ship, no, not a ship, a dinghy, heading to Lampedusa, Italy. About four hours into the journey the ship was in distress and sent out signals. The signals were received, at least one passenger was, and despite being spotted by many parties, military and commercial, the occupants of the ship were not rescued but were allowed to drift for over two weeks until only 9 of the passengers remained alive when it landed back on Libyan shores. Rescuers and the rescued report that one French warship "came so close that the migrants—on the brink of starvation—could see sailors peering at them through binoculars and taking photos."(Walt 2012; see also Forensic Architecture Project The Left-To-Die Boat 2011)

In the aftermath of those deaths, those murders, of sixty-three Africans in great distress on board the boat now known as the "left-to-die boat," a group of "researchers, architects, artists, filmmakers, activists, and theorists" started the Forensic Architecture project at Goldsmiths, University of London. They write, "Our investigations provide evidence for international prosecution teams, political organizations, NGOs, and the United Nations. Additionally, the project undertakes critical examinations of the history and present status of forensic practices in articulating notions of public truth" (Forensic Oceanography).

As part of this work the Forensic Architecture team locates the geopolitical circumstances that compel migrants to make these journeys. "In response to the Libyan uprising, an international coalition launched a military intervention in the country. As of March 23, 2011, NATO started enforcing an arms embargo off the coast of Libya. During the period of the events of the 'left-to-die boat' case, the central Mediterranean Sea was being monitored with unprecedented scrutiny, enabling NATO and participating states to become aware of any distress of migrants—and therefore be effective in assisting them. The Forensic Oceanography report turned the knowledge generated through surveillance means into evidence of responsibility for the crime of non-assistance" (Forensic Architecture Project 2012).

The ongoing crisis of capital in the form of migrants fleeing lives made unlivable is becoming more and more visible, or, perhaps, less and less able to be ignored. Think of the thousands of migrants rescued and those who have been allowed to die at sea over the course of the year 2015. The crisis is often framed as one of refugees fleeing internal economic stress and internal conflicts, but subtending this crisis is the crisis of capital and the wreckage from the continuation of military and other colonial projects of US/European wealth extraction and immiseration.

On May 18, 2015, the European Union (EU) voted to replace humanitarian patrols of the Mediterranean with military ones.[32] Under this new plan, and with Libyan cooperation that is "complicated by the fact that there is not just one government in Libya," the boats of the smugglers will be intercepted and then destroyed." The EU say that their "aim is to disrupt the business model that makes people-smuggling across the Mediterranean such a lucrative trade."[33] But the EU has no intention of disrupting the other business models, profitable to multinational corporations, that set those people flowing.

As it appears here, I mark the Forensic Architecture group's use of mapping, survivor testimony, and counternarrative as another kind of wake work that might counter forgetting, erasure, the monumental, and that ditto ditto in the archives.

Since leaving was never voluntary, return was, and still may be, an intention,
however deeply buried. There is, as it says no way in; no return.

—Dionne Brand, *A Map to the Door of No Return*

arc: noun: any unbroken part of the circumference of a circle or other curve.
verb: move with a curving trajectory.
ark: noun: *a*: a boat or ship held to resemble that in which Noah and his family
were preserved from the Flood
b: something that affords protection and safety

—Dictionary.com

What does it mean to return? Is return possible? Is it desired? And
if it is, under what conditions and for whom? The haunt of the ship
envelops and persists in the contemporary. French President Jacques
Hollande "returned" when he began his trip to the Antilles on May
10, 2015, with a visit to Guadeloupe for the opening ceremony and the
dedication of a "museum and memorial site to honour the memory of
slaves and their struggles in the French Caribbean island of Guadeloupe," the "first of its kind by France to remember those who suffered
during the slave trade." The Memorial ACTe, housed in a former sugar
factory in the Guadeloupian city of Pointe-à-Pitre, is called "a place of
remembrance and reconciliation" and described as "a Caribbean centre
on the expression and memory of slavery and the slave trade."[34]

Hollande's visit to the site spotlighted, for those who would not
and did not know, the ongoing reparation claims made by descendants
of enslaved peoples in Guadeloupe, in Haiti, Cuba, and all over the
Caribbean. And while in 2013, Hollande acknowledged France's "debt"
to Africa because of slavery and the "baneful role played by France,"
he added that this history "cannot be the subject of a transaction."[35]
Unless, of course, that transaction benefits France (like the indemnity
Haiti was forced to pay) through trade and other contracts and "in-
vestments." But what is a moral debt? How is it paid? Is it that Black
people can only be the objects of transaction and not the beneficiaries
of one, historical or not? The arc of return for Haiti is closer to a full
circle or, perhaps, that Ellisonian boomerang of history,[36] with Hollande making the first official state visit by a French president to Haiti
since its successful revolution, and with Hollande and France as the

beneficiaries of that visit and not those nations immiserated by on-going legal theft.

On March 25, 2015, on the International Day of Remembrance of the Victims of the Transatlantic Slave Trade, the United Nations dedicated *The Ark of Return* (figure 2.8). The press release read:

> The bravery of millions of victims of the transatlantic slave trade, who suffered unspeakable injustice and finally rose up to end the oppressive practice, was permanently enshrined today as the United Nations un-veiled a memorial at its New York headquarters, on the International Day of Remembrance of the Victims of Slavery and the Transatlantic Slave Trade. Entitled the *Ark of Return*, and designed by American ar-chitect Rodney Leon, of Haitian descent, the memorial aims to under-score the tragic legacy of the slave trade, which for over four centuries abused and robbed 15 million Africans of their human rights and dig-nity, and to inspire the world in the battle against modern forms of slavery, such as forced labour and human trafficking.[37]

Leon activates the familiar language of monuments and memorials: the language of injustice, suffering, tragedy, inspiration, and transcen-dence.

Rodney Leon is the architect of both *The Ark of Return* and the memorial at the African Burial Ground in Lower Manhattan, where between fifteen thousand and twenty thousand African and African-descended enslaved and free people were buried in the eighteenth cen-tury. He says *The Ark of Return* is a "good counterpoint to establish a spiritual space of return, an 'Ark of Return,' a vessel where we can begin to create a counter-narrative and undo some of that experience. The idea is that you are not necessarily returning physically, but there is a psychological, spiritual and emotional transformation, as well as a cleansing feeling through the process of moving forward to a place where humanity comes closer together."[38] What constitutes a counter-narrative here? What is the nature of this undoing?

A counter to Leon's *Ark of Return* is the work of visual and sound art-ist Charles Gaines (figures 2.14, 2.15). Gaines has been commissioned to create a temporary installation at a location on the Mississippi River, itself a gateway to Manifest Destiny, which is to say, put in service to the colonial, slave, and imperial project that was and is the United States.

Gaines has written an opera based on the cases of Dred and Harriet Scott, and he has created an installation that he calls *Moving Chains*. As he describes it, each chain link weighs ten pounds, and each chain is two hundred feet long. There are seven chains: three silver chains, a red chain in the center to represent blood, and then three additional silver chains. They are mechanized, and the silver chains move at the speed of the Mississippi, while the red chain moves at the speed of a barge on the river.

These are the coordinates of the temporary structure that Gaines calls ship-like and about which he says that being in it and walking through it will be a "ferocious experience."[39] I read Gaines's temporary monument as grounded in the knowledge of the wake, in a past that is not past, a past that is with us still; a past that cannot and should not be pacified in its presentation. Gaines's visualsonic affective language is not one of pastness and reconciliation. That river, that time, that place, are still present; the air around that ship is as disturbed as it has always been. Gaines gives us ship time, a counter to monumental time.

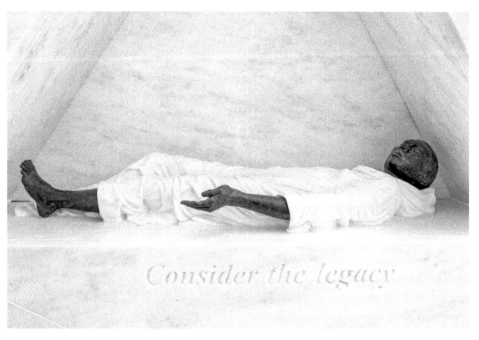

2.8 A close-up from the memorial on the legacy of slavery. Courtesy UN Photo/Devra Berkowitz

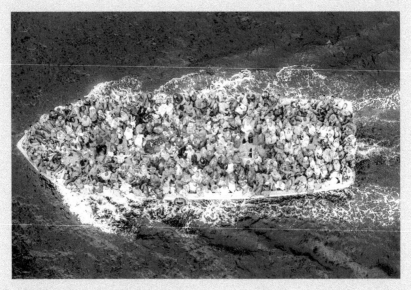

2.9 *Mare Nostrum*, June 2014. Refugees crowd on board a boat some twenty-five kilometers from the Libyan coast, prior to being rescued by an Italian naval frigate working as part of Operation Mare Nostrum. Courtesy Massimo Sestini

2.10 Operation Unified Response. © MC2(SW) Candice Villarreal/US Navy/ Handout/Corbis

2.11 Ebola cartoon. Courtesy of André Carrilho

2.12 Hew Locke, *For Those in Peril on the Sea*, 2011 (installed in the Church of St. Mary & St. Eanswythe, Folkestone). © Hew Locke. All rights reserved, DACS 2015

2.13 Romuald Hazoumè, *Lampédouzeans*, 2013. Mixed media installation, 220 × 360 × 380 cm. Image courtesy of October Gallery. © 2015 Artists Rights Society (ARS), New York / ADAGP, Paris

2.14–2.15 Renderings of *Moving Chains*, by Charles Gaines, a potential project to be located along a riverbank. Courtesy of the artist. © Charles Gaines 2015

THREE

The Hold

let me declare doorways,
corners, pursuit, let me say
standing here in eyelashes, in
invisible breasts, in the shrinking lake
in the tiny shops of untrue recollections,
the brittle gnawed life we live,
I am held, and held
—Dionne Brand, *Thirsty* (emphasis mine)

Hold—a large space in the lower part of a ship or aircraft in
which cargo is stowed. (of a ship or an aircraft); continue to follow (a particular course); keep or detain (someone); a fortress.
—OED *Online*

One cannot read the words of the second stanza of the first poem of
Dionne Brand's *Thirsty* (published in 2002, one year after *A Map to
the Door of No Return*), encounter her declaration of doorways, and
not think of those door(s) of no return all along the West Coast of
Africa. With that first poem of *Thirsty* one cannot *not* think of the ways
we, Black people in diaspora, are held and held in and by the "brittle
gnawed life we live," unprotected from the terrible except by eyelashes.
Thirsty. *Thirsty* is the final word that the poet gives to Alan as he falls . . .
dead. Readers recognize in Alan, Albert Johnson who was shot dead in
August 1979, on Manchester Avenue in Toronto; Alan Johnson, dead
from a policeman's bullet.[1] Thirsty. Thirsty on the walk, in the hold, on

the ship, on the shore and in the contemporary . . . Alan and Albert Johnson fall. We inhabit and are inhabited by the hold.

In an interview with Édouard Glissant about his theories of relation, Manthia Diawara (2011, 4) begins by saying, "A boat is a departure and an arrival." I take that duality, that doubling of departures and arrivals, as my setting-off point for this section on what happens in the hold. Charlotte Delbo's memoir *None of Us Will Return* begins with "Arrivals, Departures." Delbo reports on another kind of ship, another kind of hold, that of the cattle cars arriving at Auschwitz or Buchenwald. So she begins with the station, which is nowhere, and the door that leads to death. She writes, "But there is a station where those who arrive are those who are leaving/a station where those who arrive never have arrived, where those who have left never came back./It is the largest station in the world./This is the station" (Delbo 1995, 5). There have been earlier doors, earlier stations, earlier ports of arrival and departure; I do not include Delbo here to make an analogy between the Holocaust (Delbo was a member of the French Resistance) and slavery. Slavery's brutal arithmetics are precursive to those of the Holocaust. I begin here because of the ways Delbo makes clear that those arrivants (my word, with a nod to Brathwaite) from all over Europe, who will never depart and do not know the language of the guards, must learn a new language through kicks, punches, rifle butts, and shots. A mother slaps a child; the guards yell, hit, and pull; language falls apart.

It is in and with such falling, such ripping-apart, of language that *Zong!* begins. Language has deserted the tongue that is thirsty, it has deserted the tongues of those captives on board the slave ship *Zong* whose acquisition of new languages articulates the language of violence in the hold; the tongue struggles to form the new language; the consonants, vowels, and syllables spread across the page. The black letters float like those Africans thrown, jumped overboard, and lost in the archives and in the sea. "w w w w a wa/wa a wa t/er . . ." (Philip 2008, 3). The mouth tries to form the words of the other-tongue; except for the salty sea, water dis-appears in all of its manifestations: tears, urine, rainwater, and fresh drinking water. "One days water, water of want," Philip writes. Language disintegrates. Thirst dissolves language. If we did not know, Delbo (1995, 11) tells us: "O you who know . . . did you know that hunger makes the eyes sparkle that thirst dims/them." If we did not know, Morrison (1987, 210) tells us this in *Beloved*: "The men without skin bring us their morning water to drink we have none. . . . If we had more to drink we could make tears we cannot make sweat or morning water so the men without skin bring us theirs to drink." Danticat (1996a, 12) tells us this in "Children of the Sea" through the words of a Haitian young man dreaming of his left-behind beloved as he faces knowledge of death: "I tried to talk to you, but every time I opened my mouth, water bubbles came out. No sounds"; Brand tells us this in *Thirsty*. Together these writers elaborate the hold and its long wake, the residence time of the hold, its longue durée.

The first language the keepers of the hold use on the captives is the language of violence: the language of thirst and hunger and sore and heat, the language of the gun and the gun butt, the foot and the fist, the knife and the throwing overboard. And in the hold, mouths open, say, thirsty.

> Teenagers arriving in the Italian port of Lampedusa told workers from Save the Children how migrants from sub-Saharan African countries were often kept below the deck, deprived of water and sunlight. (Dearden 2015a)

> "The Libyans who got me to Italy are not human," he said. "They speak with the gun not with words. . . . They pushed eight Nigerians into the sea." . . . "And they pushed my friend into the sea. They all drowned." (Dearden 2015a)

> In July last year, around 100 migrants were massacred by traffickers after they tried to escape a locked hold as fumes spread from the boat's engine. As the poisonous gas spread below deck, panic started and the passengers managed to force open the door, only to be met by traffickers armed with knives who started massacring them and throwing them into the sea. (Dearden 2015a)

> "Five men stabbed and assaulted passengers at random and threw them overboard, telling others not to react or they would suffer the same fate, police said. Approximately 60 of the migrants were attacked and their bodies dumped, while around 50 are thought to have been thrown directly into the sea to drown" (Dearden 2015a). "The captain and a crew member were among only 28 survivors rescued out of the estimated 950 people on board the 66 foot former fishing trawler." (Dearden 2015b)

A teenage boy from Somalia says he wanted to be called Ali after his friend who was pushed into the sea alongside other passengers. (Dearden 2015a)

According to witness accounts gathered by police, the suspected traffickers—two Libyans, two Algerians and a Tunisian aged 21–24—threatened the migrants on board with knives and beat them with belts to control them. About 100 African migrants now presumed dead were allegedly held in the hull of the doomed boat, survivors told police. (Kirchgaessner 2015)

In the knowledges of people living in the wake these newspaper narratives have a resonance. We understand the compulsions of capital in our always-possible deaths. But those bodies nevertheless try to exceed those compulsions of capital. They, we, inhabit knowledge that the Black body is the sign of immi/a/nent death. These are accounts of the hold in the contemporary.

In Calais (figure 3.1) the keepers of the hold respond with violence as refugees from Europe's continued financialization of their unlivable lives and immiseration attempt to make it into England. Britain's prime minister, David Cameron, refers to them as a "swarm of people coming across the Mediterranean, seeking a better life, wanting to come to Britain because Britain has got jobs, it's got a growing economy, it's an incredible place to live."[2] Cameron insists on and refuses "the hold." In 2005, after uprisings in the wake of the death by electrocution of two young men who were being chased by the police, then–Interior Minister Nicolas Sarkozy referred to the young people in the streets as "scum" and "riffraff" and said that he would "Kärcher" (pressure wash) the banlieues. Cameron and Sarkozy instrumentalize the orthography of the wake. They instrumentalize the conventions of the brutal language of the hold. "Starting tomorrow, we are going to clean the Cité des 4000 with a Kärcher."[3] In Germany, in Bayreuth, Berlin, and Hamburg, the lagers continue.[4] There, refugees are held in villages for years unable to leave without permission, unable to go to the city, unable to find employment or go to school, they are in the living death of the lager. "'Being a black man or a "refugee" in Brandenburg is like being a Jew or a homosexual in the 1930's in Germany,' said Chu Eben, who fled Cameroon in 1998 and has been living in Germany ever since."[5] "Since

3.1 France-Britain-Europe migrants. © Philippe Huguen/Getty Images

late 2012, the camp at Berlin's Oranienplatz—a collection of around
30 large tents, adorned with slogans such as 'We are here' and 'Kein
mensch ist illegal' (No one is illegal)—has been home to up to 200
refugees from different parts of the world."[6] In New Orleans, Louisiana, the Black displaced of Hurricane Katrina held in deplorable conditions in the Superdome, continue to be in a holding pattern, unable to
return, unable to "move on," as the city remakes itself without them. In
Greece, on the island of Kos, police "have beaten migrants with batons
and sprayed them with fire extinguishers as hundreds were gathering at
a football stadium to wait for immigration documents."[7] On a popular
French TV program the Senegalese writer Fatou Diome said,

> These people whose bodies are washing up on these shores,—and
> I carefully choose my words—if they were Whites, the whole Earth
> should be shaking now. Instead, it's Black and Arabs who are dying
> and their lives are cheaper. The European Union, with its navy and war
> fleet, can rescue the migrants in the Atlantic and the Mediterranean
> Sea if they want to, but they sit and wait till the migrants die. It's as
> if letting them drown is used as a deterrent to prevent migrants from
> coming to Europe. But let me tell you something: that doesn't deter

anyone . . . because the individual who is migrating as a survival in-
stinct, who believes that the life they are living isn't worth much, he's
not afraid of death.[8]

The *Zong* repeats; it repeats and repeats through the logics and the
calculus of dehumaning started long ago and still operative. The details
and the deaths accumulate; the ditto ditto fills the archives of a past that
is not yet past. The holds multiply. And so does resistance to them, the
survivance of them: "*the brittle gnawed life we live, /I am held, and held.*"
We understand this because we are "*standing here in eyelashes.*"

The Belly of the Ship

What is terrifying partakes of the abyss, three times linked to the unknown.
First, the time you fell into the belly of the boat. For, in your poetic vision, a
boat has no belly; a boat does not swallow up, a boat does not devour; a boat is
steered by open skies. Yet, the belly of this boat dissolves you, precipitates you
into a nonworld from which you cry out. This boat is a womb, a womb abyss.
It generates the clamor of your protests; it also produces all coming unanimity.
Although you are alone in this suffering, you share in the unknown with others
whom you have yet to know. This boat is your womb, a matrix, and yet it ex-
pels you. This boat: pregnant with as many dead as living under the sentence
of death.

—Édouard Glissant, *Poetics of Relation*

"I attacked black terrorists, there was a black baby, they said that a black baby,
blacks in general, are terrorists. Black terror, white race." Mordechai Michael
Zaretzky, Afula, Israel (indicted for trying to kill an 18-month-old Eritrean
baby by stabbing her in the head with scissors on the evening of January 3,
2014).

—Efrat Neum, "Afula Man Indicted for Trying to Kill Black Baby"

In *Scenes of Subjection: Terror, Slavery, and Self-Making in Nineteenth
Century America* Saidiya Hartman (1997, 32) writes that "nineteenth-
century observers" of a coffle of enslaved people described that coffle
(in its formation and its movement) as "a domestic middle passage." In
"Mama's Baby, Papa's Maybe: An American Grammar Book" Hortense
Spillers writes that Africans packed into the hold of the ship were
marked according to Euro-Western definitions not as male and female

but as differently sized and weighted property. "Under these conditions," she writes, "we lose at least *gender* difference *in the outcome* and the female body and the male body become a territory of cultural and political maneuver not at all gender-related, gender-specific" (Spillers 2003b, 206; emphasis in the original).

Reading together the Middle Passage, the coffle, and, I add to the argument, the birth canal, we can see how each has functioned separately and collectively over time to dis/figure Black maternity, to turn the womb into a factory producing blackness as abjection much like the slave ship's hold and the prison, and turning the birth canal into another domestic Middle Passage with Black mothers, after the end of legal hypodescent, still ushering their children into their condition; their non/status, their non/being-ness. To confirm this we need look no farther than the postmodern orthographies of the wake—transmitted through Twitter timelines, Facebook feeds, websites, Tumblrs, Instagrams, and other online and traditional media, each organized to spectate the mothers bereft from the murders of their children, each mother forced to display her pain in public.

The birth canal of Black women or women who birth blackness, then, is another kind of domestic Middle Passage; the birth canal, that passageway from the womb through which a fetus passes during birth. *The belly of the ship births blackness; the birth canal remains in, and as, the hold.* The belly of the ship births blackness (as no/relation). Think now of those incarcerated women in the United States who are forced to give birth while shackled, their pain ignored. They are forced to deliver while shackled even when that shackling is against the law. Birthing in the belly of the state: birthed in and as the body of the state.

The slave ship, the womb and the coffle, and the long dehumaning project; we continue to feel and be the fall . . . out.

One might apprehend this dehumaning of the coffle, and with it, the birth of new "black life forms" (Rinaldo Walcott unpublished) very clearly in a description offered by four-year-old Richard in the opening pages of *Black Boy/American Hunger*. Wright (2007, 57–58) does not feel that "naked terror [he] had felt when [he] had seen the soldiers for these strange creatures were moving slowly, silently, with no suggestion of threat." He continues: "I accidentally looked down the road and saw what seemed to me to be a herd of elephants coming slowly toward me. . . . The strange elephants were a few feet from me now and I saw their faces were like the faces of men!"[9] Colin Dayan (1999, 184) begins her "Held in the Body of the State" with a similar memory: "I remember seeing, as a child growing up in Atlanta, men wearing zebra stripes working along the highway." Both Wright and Dayan elaborate the dehumaning trans*formative power of the prison and the prison coffle.

Dennis Childs fully articulates the connections between the slave ship hold, the barracoon, the prison and the prison cargo-hold. Childs excavates the "land based slave ship" used in the United States in the late nineteenth and early twentieth century:

> To fit so many prisoners into such a small space, the "cage" consisted of two parallel sections of three-tiered bunks with an access path running down the center and a hole cut in the middle of the walkway through which prisoners were forced to urinate and defecate into a bucket placed on the ground below. The outer shell of these structures was either a lattice of wooden or metal bars that left the chain-gang captive open to surveillance by camp guards and the public or four windowless wooden walls. This latter version of the rolling cage left prisoners with no view of the outside world and allowed them only a miniscule supply of breathable air—through a narrow slit running along the op of the structure. As in the case of the slave ship, the moving cage immobilized its chained prisoners to such an extent that sitting up straight was impossible.[10]

(I will return to this in "The Weather.") US incarceration rates and carceral logics directly emerging from slavery and into the present continue to be the signs that make Black bodies.

See, in figure 3.2, an image of prisoners in Malawi (2005) that evokes nothing so much as the hold of the slave ship transformed into the prison ship. The prison repeats the logics, architectural and otherwise, of the slave ship (in and across the global Black Diaspora).

With these logics in mind, I want to suggest that what is also being birthed *is* what I call *anagrammatical blackness* that exists as an index of violability and also potentiality. J. Kameron Carter (2013, 593) gets at something like this when in "Thinking with Spillers" he writes that the "'passage,' then, in 'Middle Passage' is sheer possibility and potentiality, while the 'middle' in 'Middle Passage' is . . .—existence in the middle itself." As I continue to think with Spillers's grammar, "which is

3.2 Prisoners sleep in a cell at Maula Prison just outside Lilongwe in Malawi on June 29, 2005. "The inhumanity of African prisons is a shame that hides in plain sight." © Joao Silva/The New York Times/Redux

really a rupture and a radically different kind of cultural continuation" (Spillers 2003b, 209), and Fred Moten's opening sentences in *In the Break*, that "the history of blackness is testament to the fact that objects can and do resist" and "blackness—the extended movement of a specific upheaval, an ongoing irruption that anarranges every line—is a strain that pressures the assumption of the equivalence of personhood and subjectivity" (Moten 2003, 1), I arrive at blackness as, blackness is, anagrammatical. That is, we can see the moments when blackness opens up into the anagrammatical in the literal sense as when "a word, phrase, or name is formed by rearranging the letters of another" (*Merriam-Webster Online*). We can also apprehend this in the metaphorical sense in how, regarding blackness, grammatical gender falls away and new meanings proliferate; how "the letters of a text are formed into a secret message by rearranging them" or a secret message is discovered through the rearranging of the letters of a text. *Ana-*, as a prefix, means "up, in place or time, back, again, anew."[11] So, blackness anew, blackness as a/temporal, in and out of place and time putting pressure on meaning and that against which meaning is made. We see again and again how, in and out of the United States (as my point of departure and arrival), *girl* doesn't mean "girl" but, for example, "prostitute" or "felon,"[12] *boy* doesn't mean "boy," but "Hulk Hogan" or "gunman," "thug" or "urban youth."[13] We see that *mother* doesn't mean "mother," but "felon" and "defender" and/or "birther of terror" and not one of the principal grounds of terrors multiple and quotidian enactments.[14] We see that *child* is not "child," and a Coast Guard cutter becomes, in Brathwaite's hands, a Coast Guard gutter—not a rescue or a medical ship but a carrier of coffins, a coffle, and so on.[15] As the meanings of words fall apart, we encounter again and again the difficulty of sticking the signification. This is Black being in the wake. This is the anagrammatical. These are Black lives, annotated. (I will return to what I am calling Black annotation in the final section of this work, "The Weather.")

Let us return to Aereile Jackson, the Black woman who is made simultaneously to appear and disappear in Sekula and Burch's *The Forgotten Space*—Aereile Jackson, identified as "former mother." What does it mean to be a "former mother" and, in particular, what does it mean to be a "former mother" when one has *never* been able to lay claim to *how* mother means in the world? When, as Spillers has told us, Black life is an "enforced state of breach," and mother (like family) is a relation that loses meaning *"since it can be invaded at any given and arbitrary moment by the property relations"* (Spillers 2003b, 218; emphasis in the original)? What does this phrasing of "former mother" to describe a woman whose children have been taken from her (and likely placed into "care") tell us about the afterlives of slavery and the afterlives of property? Who, or perhaps what, bears the status of non/former/un mother when one's children are lost through death or because they are "held in the body of the state," and how does one become a *former* mother? Unless, that is, the word *mother* never took hold for Black women in and then out of slavery in the "New World." We are inundated with images of Black women in pain, of Black un/mothers grieving Black un/children. In *Laboring Women* Jennifer Morgan (2004, 200) writes, "The challenge, for historians of the early Atlantic, at any rate, is to account for the equally innumerable acts of humanity, the ways in which men and women caught in the maelstrom of colonial upheavals reconfigured their subsequent sense of identity and possibility. Motherhood, for instance, cannot possibly remain unmodified when it is understood in the context of both the overwhelming commodification of the bodies of infants and their mothers, and the potential impulse women must have felt to interrupt such obscene calculations." *"Motherhood . . . cannot possibly remain unmodified."*

My friend Jemima tweets a screenshot of a series of text messages with her eleven-year-old son. He wants a bulletproof shirt. She asks him if he is okay. He says no. She says *she is sad that he thinks he needs one*; she wonders if something immediate has happened to him. He replies that *he is sorry that he needs one.* She promises him that they will protect him, that they will keep him safe. She does this knowing, before, and as, and after, she writes this, that there is a limit to what she can do to protect him; that there is no safe space and . . . still, like Denver in *Beloved*, he has to "know it, and go on out the yard. Go on" (Morrison 1987, 244). In the afterlives of partus sequitur ventrem what does, what can, mothering mean for Black women, for Black people? What kind of mother/ing is it if one must always be prepared with knowledge of the possibility of the violent and quotidian death of one's child? Is it mothering if one knows that one's child might be killed at any time in the hold, in the wake by the state no matter who wields the gun? (Spillers's every relationship invaded by the state.) Swallowed whole by the state, purged by the police, stopped and frisked, back broken, humiliated, interned in "camps" for women and children. My friend and her son are held by the state and mother and child . . . fall apart.

> *"She was a mother, she was a wife, she was mine, no longer is she mine." These are the words of Raynetta Turner's husband Herman after she was found dead in a jail cell the morning after her complaints that she felt ill were ignored. She was a mother of eight and she was in prison because she was accused of shoplifting food.*[16]

Hortense Spillers wrote in "Interstices: A Small Drama of Words" that slavery *trans*formed the Black woman, she "became, instead, the principal point of passage between the human and the non-human world" (Spillers 2003a, 155). Joy James reminds us that Thomas Jefferson, who could not see Phillis Wheatley as a poet, was "an astute consumer of black female reproductivity. In *Notes on the State of Virginia*, Jefferson differentiates between the Indigenous *social* savage and the African biological or *ontological* savage. He illustrates with bestiary: orangutans, he asserts, prefer black women. Jefferson exempts all other racially subjugated human forms from animalized sexuality (e.g., he does not opine that female orangutans prefer black males or buffalos desire Native women)" (James 2014, 127). Spillers writes in "Mama's Baby, Papa's Maybe" that Africans were not only ungendered in Middle Passage, marked not as male and female but as differently sized and weighted property: "Female in 'Middle Passage,' as the apparently smaller physical mass, occupies 'less room' in a directly translatable money economy. But she is, nevertheless, quantifiable by the same rules of accounting as her male counterpart" (Spillers 2003b, 215). And, again, it is Hartman (1997, 32) who reminds us in *Scenes of Subjection* that the coffle, which reappears as the chain gang in and out of slavery, "was described by nineteenth-century observers as a domestic middle passage, piracy, a momentous evil, and most frequently, a crime."

We see in many visual and other representations in public life, certainly in the United States, but as the quotation from the man from Afula, Israel, that began this section indicates, not only in the United States, Black people ejected from the state become the national symbols for the less-than-human being condemned to death; become the *carriers* of terror, terror's embodiment (*an* internal, *the* internal terroristic threat) and not the primary objects of terror's multiple enactments but the ground of terror's possibility. There is an extensive representational repertoire (photographic and discursive) of the conflation of blackness and death and multiple "commonsense" representations of Black maternity—and therefore the impossibility of Black childhood—as condemning one to a life of violence. We trace this history back to chattel slavery and the law of partus sequitur ventrem (again, "that which is brought forth follows the womb"), which dictated that the children of a slave woman inherited the mother's non/status. Black women and children continue to be cast as less-than-human *victims* and *agents* of "natural" disasters, whether in the aftermath of the 2010 Haitian earthquake, a boat sinking during a perilous journey, or Hurricane Katrina. On October 29, 2012, on Staten Island, New York, Glenda Moore looked for and was refused shelter during Hurricane Sandy. That particular refusal resulted in the drowning deaths of her sons Connor and Brendan, aged two and four, and her condemnation by many as an unfit mother. What, they demand, was she doing out in that storm? What kind of mother was she? Not only that, but when the white man who denied her shelter was asked why he didn't open the door to that distraught Black woman who repeatedly pounded on it for help, he said that he did not see a Black woman at all but a BIG Black man and that he was *forced*, therefore, to spend the night with his back against the door to prevent entry and thereby his own violation.[17] "*in the beginning the women are away from the men and the men are away from the women storms rock us and mix the men into the women and the women into the men*" (Morrison 1987, 211).

What is a Black child? In the United States, conservatives simultaneously call for an end to abortion and extoll the imagined virtues of it. Recall Bill Bennett, former US Secretary of Education and "values czar": "If it were your sole purpose to reduce crime," Bennett said, "You could abort every black baby in this country, and your crime rate would go down."[18] This is an execrable arithmetic, a violent accounting. Another indication that the meaning of *child*, as it abuts blackness, falls . . . apart.

An early instance of recognition of what I am calling anagrammatical blackness appears clearly and most literally in Frederick Douglass's shift from Aunt Hester in the 1845 *Narrative of the Life of Frederick Douglass* to Aunt Esther in the 1855 *My Bondage and My Freedom*. Because as much as Douglass has painstakingly elaborated the violences, the everyday tyranny, and resistances of Hester's and his own lives in slavery in which any white person has the right to demand anything of her (and him), once Hawthorne publishes *The Scarlet Letter* in 1850 Hester is tied to the grammar of the human in civil society who can contravene the law; the human who is able to consent, even if she is punished for doing so. In addition, then, to the literal anagrammatical (the same letters, rearranged) of Hester into Esther in Douglass, I am thinking of blackness's signifying surplus: the ways that meaning slides, signification slips, when words like *child*, *girl*, *mother*, and *boy* abut blackness. Think again of the multiple studies that tell us that though known to be in pain, Black people are "forced to endure more pain" and that Black children are consistently seen as being older than they are and are therefore, never really considered children.[19] Turn, in the United States, to the recent 2015 news story that described a white eighteen-year-old young man and a thirteen-year-old white girl child both fugitives from the law who stole cars, forged and stole checks, crossed state lines, and were armed, as "Bonnie and Clyde" and as "teenage sweethearts." They did not describe the man as a predator and the girl as a prostitute (as the two likely would have been described had they been Black), nor did they describe the pair as felons or as criminals who were armed and dangerous. No. This white pair was thrown a lifeline (not the buoy of those Black people beheld in Brathwaite's *Dream Haiti*) that extended to them a grammar that cohered in and around the human. They were extended a narrative that worked to make them legible and largely sympathetic.[20] It was a narrative that first diminished the fact of, and then later the severity of, the many "criminal acts" that they committed; this narrative rearranged crime into romance.[21]

Think now of the recent article that described *seven-year-old* Aiyana Stanley-Jones as a sleeping, unarmed seven-year-old.[22] Stanley-Jones was murdered in 2010 by Officer Joseph Weekley, a white Detroit police officer who, accompanied by a SWAT team and the crew of the television show *48 Hours*, arrived at the door where seven-year-old Aiyana lived with her grandmother and other family members. With prior knowledge that the person they were looking for lived upstairs, the police nevertheless burst into her home and threw a flash grenade. Aiyana was asleep on the sofa in the living room; the grenade set her blanket on fire and she was severely burned. Then Weekley fired his gun (a submachine gun),[23] and the bullet struck Aiyana in the head and killed her. Despite the establishment of these facts, all charges eventually were dropped against Weekley. *Unarmed. Sleeping. Seven years old.* What are we to make of this conjunction of a seven-year-old, sleeping, and unarmed? Are we to approach these terms as if they make sense outside of the il/logics of colonization, outside of the il/logic of Black life in the wake, outside of the il/logic of being armed with blackness? When her grandmother addressed Weekley she said, "I get no sleep. I am sick. I am sick as hell. I get no sleep. The flashbacks. I wouldn't wish this on nobody in the world. Not even you."[24]

Wake: in the line of recoil of (a gun). Wake: the state of wakefulness or consciousness.

Think of Mikia Hutchings (to whom I will return later in "The Weather"), a Black twelve-year-old girl child, caught with her white girlfriend writing on a school wall, faced with a possible felony because her family was unable to pay the hundred-dollar restitution fine. A felony for writing on a school wall, but one that can be avoided if one has sufficient money. I could go on. These stories, too, accumulate; the ditto ditto in the archives of the present.

Think of the second autopsy ordered by the family of Michael Brown—the annotated autopsy report that shows the extent of his injuries. These necessary annotations were made by the medical examiner hired by the family to prove that there *was* injury and the extent of it; to show, in the face of the readily adopted language of black monstrosity embedded in the language of "strong-arm robbery," that he was not armed; to show that he was fleeing and gravely injured. Listen to how Darren Wilson's grand jury testimony evacuates *his* role as "strong arm" of the law and state power falls away as the armed and trained cop is transformed by his proximity to blackness into a five-year-old child.

> "When I grabbed him [Michael Brown, the unarmed 19-year-old young Black man], the only way I can describe it is I felt like a five-year-old holding onto Hulk Hogan. . . . When he looked at me, he made like a grunting, like aggravated sound and he starts, he turns and he's coming back towards me," Wilson recalled. "His first step is coming towards me, he kind of does like a stutter step to start running. When he does that, his left hand goes in a fist and goes to his side, his right one goes under his shirt in his waistband and he starts running at me."
>
> "He was almost bulking up to run through the shots, like it was making him mad that I'm shooting him," Wilson said. "And the face that he had was looking straight through me, like I wasn't even there, I wasn't even anything in his way." Wilson took aim at Brown's head for the shot that would kill the unarmed teen. "When he fell, he fell on his face," Wilson recalled. "I remember his feet coming up . . . and then they rested."[25]

Darren Wilson has a brutal mythical imagination. Here is Cornelius Eady in *Brutal Imagination*, on the Susan Smith case. Smith drowned her two sons (ages three and fourteen months) in 1995 in Union, South Carolina, and then accused a Black man, a specter, *the* specter, of the crime. In "How I Got Born," when Eady (2001, 5) writes, he could be writing of Darren Wilson and more:

Though it's common belief
That Susan Smith willed me alive
At the moment her babies sank into the lake.
When called, I come.
My job is to get things done.
.   .   .   .
Susan Smith has invented me because
Nobody else in town will do what
She needs me to do.
I mean: jump in an idling car
And drive off with two sad and
Frightened kids in the back.
Like a bad lover she has given me a poisoned heart.
It pounds both our ribs, black, angry, nothing but business.
Since her fear is my blood
And her need part mythical,
everything she says about me is true.
Who are you, mister?
One of the boys asks
From the eternal back seat
And here is the one good thing:
if I am alive, then so, briefly are they.

Michael Brown is Darren Wilson's projection, as the unknown Black man in Susan Smith's case is hers. The hold, the middle of Canfield Drive in Ferguson, Missouri, is lit and filled with and by brutal imagination. And so is the stop.

The Stop

> In the Diaspora, as in bad dreams, you are constantly overwhelmed by the persistence of the spectre of captivity.
> —Dionne Brand, *A Map to the Door of No Return*

Carding, stop-and-frisk, family detention centers, holding centers, *Lager*, quarantine zones . . . are other names by which one might recognize the hold as it appears in Calais, Toronto, New York City, Haiti, Lampedusa, Tripoli, Sierra Leone, Bayreuth, and so on.

In December 2011 the *New York Times* ran an op-ed piece, "Why Is the N.Y.P.D. after Me?," by Nicholas K. Peart. It begins: "When I was 14, my mother told me not to panic if a police officer stopped me. And she cautioned me to carry ID and never run away from the police or I could be shot. In the nine years since my mother gave me this advice, I have had numerous occasions to consider her wisdom" (Peart 2011). With the ongoing murders of Black people in the United States, for driving, walking, asking for help, and breathing while Black, this is good advice; this is necessary advice from a Black mother to her Black son, and it is still, and has been, insufficient to the force that he meets in the world.

When the *New York Times* subsequently ran an article in July 2012 about Black women who are subject to stop-and-frisk on the streets of New York City, the focus was on their belief that in the course of those stops they were shamed and improperly touched. The article tells us that "the laws governing street stops are blind to gender" and that "when conducting a frisk, police officers in New York are trained in the Patrol Guide to slide their hands over the external clothing, focusing on 'the waistband, armpit, collar and groin areas.' . . . The training does not draw a distinction between male and female suspects" (Ruderman 2012). This means that whoever is stopped and frisked by those authorized to do so is handled without regard for gender distinction, without consent, and they are liable to be sexually violated.

> Shari Archibald's black handbag sat at her feet on the sidewalk in front of her Bronx home on a recent summer night. The two male officers crouched over her leather bag and rooted around inside, elbow-deep. One officer fished out a tampon and then a sanitary napkin, crinkling the waxy orange wrapper between his fingers in search of drugs. Next he pulled out a tray of foil-covered pills, Ms. Archibald recalled. "What's this?" the officer said, examining the pill packaging stamped "drospirenone/ethinylestradiol." "Birth control," Ms. Archibald remembered saying. She took a breath and exhaled deeply, hoping the whoosh of air would cool her temper and contain her humiliation as the officers proceeded to pat her down. (Ruderman 2012)

> Male officers are permitted to frisk a woman if they reasonably suspect that she may be armed with a dangerous weapon that could be used to harm them. *A frisk can escalate into a field search* if officers feel a suspi-

cious bulge while patting down the woman's outer layer of clothing or the outline of her purse. (Ruderman 2012, emphasis mine)

"Yes, it's intrusive, but wherever a weapon can be concealed is where the officer is going to search," Inspector Royster said. That search is not random; it is based on information provided to an officer, like a detailed description of an armed suspect, or actions that raise an officer's reasonable suspicion that the woman may be armed, she added. And although the police stops of women yielded very few guns, they did produce 3,993 arrests last year. "Safety has no gender," Inspector Royster said. "When you are talking about the safety of an officer, the first thing he or she is going to do is mitigate that threat." (Ruderman 2012)

Here is the rubric of the stop: "furtive movements, carrying suspicious object, casing a victim or location, fits a relevant description, suspect acting as a lookout, actions indicative of a drug transaction, other, actions of engaging in a violent crime, suspicious bulge, wearing clothes commonly used in a crime. . . ."[26] Might we read in the case of "suspicious bulge" yet another policing of gender categories, of terrorizing Black men and women across sex and gender? The records revealed "a teenager forcibly handcuffed for concealing an erection."[27] "Crystal Pope, 22, said she and two female friends were frisked by male officers last year in Harlem Heights. The officers said they were looking for a rapist." She reports, "They tapped around the waistline of my jeans. . . . They tapped the back pockets of my jeans, around my buttock. It was kind of disrespectful and degrading. It was uncalled-for. It made no sense. *How are you going to stop three females when you are supposedly looking for a male rapist?*" (emphasis mine). Women friends stopped and frisked by cops looking for a male rapist; terrorized in the name of protecting women, not acknowledged to be women, from terror. Once again, in these spaces of terror, heteronormative Euro-gender relations disappear *in the outcome*.

Peart makes clear in his article the radically and racially restricted spaces in and through which Black men and women, girls and boys—stopped and frisked at a rate of almost seven hundred thousand in 2011—can live and move unimpeded. Stop-and-frisk is one rite of passage that marks the space/race/place of no rights and no citizenship (à la *Dred Scott v. Sanford* [1857]) in one direction and, in the other, the space through which the rights to free passage are secured for non-blacks. The free papers return here. And if, since, it is a rite of passage—indicative of no rights, no citizenship à la the *Dred Scott* decision—one must ask what it marks passage from, through, and to. Peart (2011) continues, "Police are far more likely to use force when stopping blacks or Latinos than whites. In half the stops police cite the vague 'furtive movements' as the reason for the stop." As another young Black man reports, "When you're young and you're black, no matter how you look you fit the description."[28] You "fit the description" of the nonbeing, the being out of place, and the noncitizen always available to and for death.

The reality and the provenance of policing and stop-and-frisk's language of "furtive movements" follow a direct line from the overseer and the slave master/ slave owner's and any white persons' charge of impudence as "one of the commonest and most indefinite in the whole catalogue of offenses usually laid to the charge of slaves" (Douglass [1855] 2003a, 92). Maintaining that stop-and-frisk "saves lives," on two consecutive Sundays in June 2012 former New York City mayor Michael Bloomberg took that case to predominantly Black churches, where he told the congregants, "The city would not 'deny reality' in order to stop different groups according to their relative proportions in the population."[29] We must ask whose lives are being saved, who in fact is in possession of a life that can be saved, because it is clear that in at least one direction Black lives are being destroyed. According to Frederick Douglass ([1855] 2003a, 92), "Whatever it is, or is not . . . this offense [imprudence] may be committed in various ways; in the tone of an answer; in answering at all; in not answering; in the expression of countenance; in the motion of the head; in the gait, manner and bearing of the slave." Likewise, whatever furtive movements are or are not, any movements while Black may be interpreted as furtive. Think of Trayvon Martin and Chavis Carter. Also think of the arrest of Monica Jones for walking while Black and transgender, and the arrest and prosecution of the New Jersey Four. Pause there, for a moment, on the New Jersey Four. Four out of a group of seven young Black lesbians who faced felony charges, who were found guilty of second-degree gang assault, and who were sentenced to and served all or part of from three and a half to eleven years in prison, because they protected themselves and each other from a Black male attacker who threatened to "fuck them straight."[30] Think, too, of the shooting death of nineteen-year-old Renisha McBride, a young Black woman who was in a car accident in the early hours of the morning and who went looking for assistance at a house in Detroit's white suburb. Instead of help she was met with a fatal gunshot wound to the face. Think again of Miriam Carey, Glenda Moore, Jordan Dunn, Tamir Rice, Jonathan Holloway, Sandra Bland, Eric Garner, Jonathan Crawford, Rekia Boyd, Yvette Smith, Laquan McDonald, and many more.

Over 90 percent of the stops in New York in 2011 were of men, and the accounts of stop-and-frisk focus largely on their experiences. The NYPD has another stop-and-frisk program known as Operation Clean Halls ("the only one of its kind in a major U.S. city that gives police standing permission to roam the halls of private buildings")[31] that targets and polices women, children, *and* men and that has effectively placed "hundreds of thousands of New Yorkers, mostly black and Latino, under siege in their own homes."[32] As *part* of their mandate *and as an effect of it* these programs surveil, restrict, and pathologize Black women's and men's expressions and performances of sexuality and desire. One young Black man reports that after being stopped and frisked, he was dismissed by the police with the admonition "Stay safe." "Stay safe?" he asks, "After he just did all that?"[33]

"Cradle to Grave," Womb to Tomb

> Cradle to grave: From creation to disposal; throughout the life cycle. The term is used in a number of business contexts, but most typically in company's responsibility for dealing with hazardous waste and product performance. Same as "womb to tomb." See also "manifest system."
> —*Business Dictionary Online*

I ask again, borrowing Philip's phrase, what does it look like to "defend the dead"? The first-grade teacher in Paterson, New Jersey, posts on Facebook that she thinks of her students as "future criminals."[34] "Future criminal" joins "former mother" in the anagrammatical: not child; not mother; not being. In the wake, we must connect the birth industry to the prison industry, the machine that degrades and denies and eviscerates reproductive justice to the machine that incarcerates. On February 6, 2013, the Education section of the *New York Times* published an article titled "A Hospital Offers a Grisly Lesson on Gun Violence." The article begins, "In a darkened classroom, 15 eighth graders gasped as a photograph appeared on the screen in front of them. It showed a dead man whose jaw had been destroyed by a shotgun blast, leaving the lower half of his face a shapeless, bloody mess."[35] The fifteen middle school students present on this particular day are largely Black, and they are participants in a program at Temple University Hospital in North Philadelphia called Cradle to Grave, or C2G. The Cradle to Grave program announces itself: "In response to the increased number of homicides involving young people, Temple University Hospital has created a *highly interactive, two-hour experience* that confronts participants with the realities of youth violence on a personal level" (emphasis mine).[36] Do we understand "cradle to grave" here as a command or as a description of Black life lived, as I have argued, always in the present tense of death? Likewise, "participant" can be the correct word to describe the children in attendance only if we hear and feel in it Frederick Douglass's description of himself as "witness and participant" to his Aunt Hester's beating, his knowledge that that is also his fate, his certainty that *his* entrance through slavery's violent "blood-stained gate" (Douglass ([1845] 2003a, 44) is imminent. We read that Cradle to Grave "brings in youths from across Philadelphia in the hope that an unflinching look at the effects that guns have in their community will deter young people from reaching for a gun to settle personal scores, and will help them recognize that gun violence is not the glamorous business sometimes depicted in television shows and rap music" (Hurdle 2013).

In Cradle2Grave's logo, the numeral 2 appears an un/conscious doubling, a redoubling, a signifier of how for many in the wake the cradle and the grave continue to be produced as the same space. It is a reminder that to be Black is to be continually produced by the wait toward death; that the cradle and the grave double as far as Black flesh is concerned.

Telling the story of Lamont Adams, a Black adolescent, who was sixteen years old when he was murdered, Cradle to Grave exposes children, many of whom are already experiencing trauma *from their material, lived violence,* to photos and reenactments of graphic violence as a deterrent to more violence. We read, "As the 13- and 14-year-olds gathered around a gurney on a recent visit, Mr. Charles told the story of Lamont Adams, 16, who died at the hospital after being shot 14 times by another boy" (Hurdle 2013). One young person is invited to put her body in the s/place of Lamont Adams's body, on the gurney that he would have been placed on (figure 3.3). "The vicarious experience the program provides succeeds in creating these 'teachable moments' that are comparable to those awakened in actual trauma patients."[37] How are we to understand trauma here? These young people's bodies are always already in the space of Lamont Adams's body; it is not that step *into the hold* that requires imagination.

Charles, the hospital's trauma outreach coordinator, says that in the program's seven-and-a-half-year history, no parent has ever complained that their child was shown these images. This statement does less to reassure readers, or at least this reader, of the correctness or appropriateness of the program than it does to portray childhood while poor and Black as abandonment. I would wager that those same doctors and administrators would not want *their* early teenaged son or daughter exposed to such graphic violence. I would wager that they would not consider it simply an "education" or a "teachable moment" for their child to be positioned face down on an empty body bag and tagged with orange dots to mark each of the twenty-four points of entry and exit for the bullets that struck, and eventually killed, sixteen-year-old Lamont Adams.

From Phillis onward, because Black children are not seen as children and the corral of "urban youth" holds them outside of the category of the child, they are offered more trauma by the state and state actors and not the therapy that the following Alex Kotlowitz quotation from another Philadelphia program illustrates as necessary. And they are certainly not offered the new world or ways toward imagining it that their, that our, circumstances demand.

Alex Kotlowitz writes in the *New York Times* about another program in Philadelphia called Healing Hurt People: Center for Nonviolence and Social Justice.[38] At least in name Healing Hurt People acknowledges "people" and "hurt" and aims for social justice and an end to violence, including the violence of exposing those who live in and with violence to more violence. Healing Hurt People seems to acknowledge that trauma, the bow of the ship, leaves something in its wake.

> As Dr. Corbin and his colleagues began to work with shooting victims in Philadelphia, they saw clear symptoms of post-traumatic stress

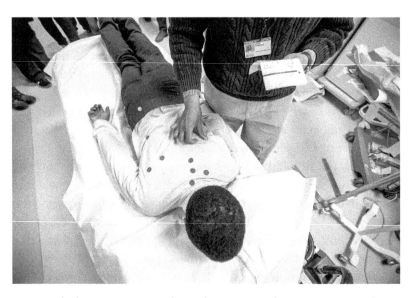

3.3 Scott Charles, a trauma outreach coordinator at Temple University Hospital, places red stickers on Justin Robinson, thirteen, an eighth grader from Kenderton School, to show the bullet wounds suffered by Lamont Adams, a local teenager who died violently in 2004, during the Cradle to Grave program at the hospital in Philadelphia, February 1, 2013. The program brings in youths with the hope that a look at the effects of gunshot wounds can help them reject gun violence. © Jessica Kourkounis / The New York Times / Redux

> disorder. I visited the program last summer and met one young man who had night terrors so real that his girlfriend feared for her safety. Another young man told me that whenever he passes the spot where he was shot, he thinks he sees himself on the ground writhing in pain, and he approaches the specter to assure himself that he'll be O.K. Another who was shot and paralyzed in an argument over a pair of sunglasses said that whenever he thinks about revenge or gets angry, which is often, he has incapacitating phantom pains in his legs. Two of the young men I spoke to had attempted suicide. Virtually all spoke of feeling alone, of not trusting anyone. (Kotlowitz 2013)

The hold repeats and repeats and repeats in and into the present, into the classroom and the hospital.

In December 2013, the *New York Times* ran a front-page feature called "Invisible Child: Dasani's Homeless Life in the Shadows" (Elliott

2013). As it stands, the series is as much an exposé of Dasani Coates's "inheritance" of a life of precarity because of the "bad choices" of a parent (primarily her mother) as it is of the massive and systemic failures of programs set up to address poverty and homelessness. The feature focused on Dasani Coates,[39] an eleven- and then twelve-year-old Black girl child, and her family (seven siblings and two parents), who live in one of New York City's family shelters.[40] (*Family* falls apart, in the wake of the hold and the ship, it cannot hold.) In part 1 of the series, readers are introduced to Dasani at home and as she makes her way to the Susan S. McKinney Secondary School of the Arts ("A Place Where Hope Begins & Dreams Come True")—a school whose already tight space, we read, may be made even tighter with its impending displacement from its third-floor performance spaces by a(n unwanted and contested) charter school.

Once the narrative brings us into the school, we are introduced to Ms. Holmes, the principal of the McKinney School, who is described as a formidable woman. A "towering woman, by turns steely and soft," Ms. Holmes "wears a Bluetooth like a permanent earring and tends toward power suits. She has been at McKinney's *helm* for 15 years and runs *the school like a naval ship, peering down its gleaming hallways as if searching the seas for enemy vessels. . . .* She leaves her office door permanently open, *like a giant, unblinking eye*" (Elliott 2013, emphasis mine). Martial metaphors and the language of surveillance subtend the logics of the hold. The woman and the school-as-ship both are described as sanctuaries *and* sites of surveillance.[41] Dasani's homeroom has "inspirational words" like "Success does not come without sacrifice" (Elliott 2013). What brutal imagination positions a site of surveillance as a sanctuary and for whom? But who and what are to be sacrificed for such "success[es]," but on whose and what terms? Reading that Ms. Holmes suspends Dasani for a week for fighting, we are to understand that for Dasani, already homeless, "to be suspended is to be *truly* homeless" (Elliott 2013, emphasis mine). It is maritime and martial metaphors like ships, success, struggle, sacrifice, and surveillance that activate this narrative of Dasani Coates, invisible child. (I wrote "inviable" instead of "invisible" child, a mistake that is not a mistake because surely to be an invisible child is also to be an inviable child, and as phrases they both appear alongside that earlier sobriquet "former mother" attached to Aereile Jackson.) Dasani is another little girl with the word *Ship* on her forehead.

As Wynter (2006, emphasis mine) has told us: *"The function of the curriculum is to structure what we call 'consciousness,' and therefore certain behaviors and attitudes."* And these certain curricular attitudes structure our, all of our, consciousness.

Education in the belly of the ship. Dasani's narrative is one of her instruction in how to live in a world that demands her death, and it is used as curriculum. That is, not only does the "Invisible Child" series feature the education of Dasani but it is, itself, featured in the *Times* Education section, as this series becomes part of a larger curriculum as a narrative of individual resilience and overcoming—a "Teaching and Learning with the New York Times" that consists of the traumatizing and retraumatizing of Black children for the education of others. Traumatized children being forced to endure more trauma; children in pain being subjected to more pain.[42] Both the school and the woman at its head are described as ships, ships in the storm. But we, in the wake, must acknowledge the ship *as* the storm. Recall Morrison's Sethe and the Haitian girl child with the word *Ship* affixed to her forehead so that we might ask again: *How can the very system that is designed to unmake and inscribe her also be the one to save her?* How can the one marked *by* the ship (see figure 2.5) be saved by being marked *for* it?

Elliott's article initiated a new wave of criticism of Michael Bloomberg: that during his three terms as mayor, New York City's rates of homelessness, particularly among families and young people, climbed higher than they had been in decades. Outgoing mayor Bloomberg denied that these problems were systemic. "This kid [Dasani] was dealt a bad hand," Bloomberg said. *"I don't know quite why. That's just the way God works. Sometimes some of us are lucky and some of us are not"* (emphasis mine).[43]

On January 1, 2014, the *Guardian* published a "Comment Is Free" piece written by a young Black man identified by a picture and the first name William.[44] William, who is seventeen and a junior in high school, identifies himself as one of the twenty-two thousand homeless children in New York City, and he speaks to the tremendous difficulties he has faced in and out of school because of the material and psychic toll of chronic homelessness. Framed as a direct response to Andrea Elliott's *New York Times* profile of Dasani and also to Michael Bloomberg's comments, William outlined a series of failures when he wrote, "I don't think I was dealt a bad hand in life, but I think I was passed a bad hand from my mother. But it's OK because she also slid an ace down my wrist and told me to save it. She is the ace. As long as she's there, no matter how terrible my hand is, we make it through."[45] William is a young man without access to a structural critique of poverty. Though he makes use of Bloomberg's language of the bad hand, he also inserts something else, some other knowledge, into that space. Unlike Bloomberg, who denies the existence of the hold, William says that this bad hand was not dealt directly to him (or, by extension, to Dasani). In other words, *he* wasn't in the game, *he* didn't make that choice; the hand was passed to him by his mother, who also slipped him "an ace" (a salvation, in her continued presence, her continued support). Put another way, William lays both the fault of *needing* knowledge of/for survival *and* the acquisition of that knowledge necessary for survival squarely at his mother's feet. His education is in the hold, and because of it he accounts for being held by the state and also by his mother. In *"the brittle gnawed life we live, / I am held, and held."*

To return briefly to Philadelphia and to Temple University Hospital's Cradle2Grave program: as the students hear about Lamont Adams's horrible death, Mr. Charles tells them that "the wounds he finds most moving were those in the boy's hands. 'He holds up his hands and begs the boy to stop shooting. . . . He [the boy] had not prepared himself for how terrible this would be.' As the details of Lamont's story unfolded, one girl struggled to keep her composure. Another hid her face in her friend's shoulder. Lamont died about 15 minutes after arriving at the hospital." Following these graphic details, Dr. Goldberg concludes the lesson with a question. *"Who,"* she asks, *"do you think has the best chance of saving your life?"* Her answer? *"You do'"* (Hurdle 2013). I read in this question, as it arrives at the end of a graphic display of Black suffering, a narrative condemnation of "urban youth"; a wholesale abandonment of Black children to their own devices; a making manifest under the guise of education of the lives of Black children, not seen as children, being in their own hands as they face a series of catastrophes "unprepared for how terrible this would be." *Wake; in the line of recoil of (a gun).*

When we reach the end of "Invisible Child," we read that Dasani Coates imagines herself designing her own video game. We read that if she could "she would call it 'Live or Die' and the protagonist would be an 11-year-old girl fighting for her own salvation" (Elliott 2013).

In the midst of the ongoing willful disasters of the wake and as part of their resistance to them, in 2013 the Black Youth Project and a group of Black scholar activists drafted and circulated a petition in order to get President Obama to go to Chicago to address the violence there *and to and speak to and stand with Black and Brown people*, in the devastation being wrought in his adopted hometown.[46] The scholars and activists who wrote and circulated the petition did so in the (misplaced) hope that if he answered the call of many in the Black community to, "Come home, Mr. President, your city needs you," that he would *manifest* the same compassion, the same feeling for and with, that he showed in Newtown, Connecticut. They hoped that by "coming to Chicago, coming to the south and west side of Chicago, [he would] signal to the country that the loss of the families in Chicago is just as important to us as a nation as the loss of young people in suburban areas."[47] I want to hold onto the multiple meanings of *manifest* here as in "plain" or "obvious," manifesto, and the list of a ship's cargo. With my use of *manifest* here I am specifically attuned to the listing of enslaved Africans as cargo, the absence of personhood indicated by space in the hold, the space of the word *ditto* taking the place of a given name, the way that in the section titled "Os" in *Zong!* Philip insists on her own underwriting by providing at the bottom of the page names for the enslaved, those thrown and jumped overboard.

In the immediate aftermath of the murders of twenty children and six adults at Sandy Hook Elementary School in Newtown, Connecticut, and at the vigil there on December 16, 2012, a visibly shaken President Obama stepped up to the microphone to deliver words of "comfort and love from across the U.S." and the message that "*'we' can only keep kids safe together.*" It is with great difficulty and a sense of responsibility that in the speech the president calls the name of each child and each adult murdered in that school. "This job," he says,

> of keeping our children safe and teaching them well is something we can only do together. . . . In that way we come to realize that we bear responsibility for each other. . . . *Can we honestly say that we're doing enough to keep our children, all of them, safe from harm?* Can we claim, as a nation, that we're all together there, letting them know they are loved and teaching them to love in return? Can we say that we're truly

doing *enough to give all the children of this country* the chance they deserve to live out their lives in happiness and with purpose? I've been reflecting on this the last few days, and if we're honest with ourselves, the answer's no. We're not doing enough. And we will have to change. ... *If there's even one step we can take to save another child* or another parent or another town from the grief that's visited Tucson and Aurora and Oak Creek and Newtown and communities from Columbine to Blacksburg before that, then surely we have an obligation to try. (Emphasis mine)

He continues: "In the coming weeks, I'll use whatever power this office holds to engage my fellow citizens, from law enforcement, to mental health professionals, to parents and educators, in an effort aimed at preventing more tragedies like this, because what choice do we have?"[48]

On January 29, 2013, Hadiya Pendleton, a fifteen-year-old Black girl, a Chicago high school student, was murdered in Chicago, one week after she performed at Obama's second inauguration. On February 12, 2013, President Obama delivered his fifth State of the Union address to a joint session of the US Congress.[49] Obama calls Hadiya Pendleton's name in his State of the Union address and places her death in the context of the gun deaths and the mass murders committed, largely, by white men in the United States, and the recent stripping away of parts of the Voting Rights Act. He says,

In the two months since Newtown, more than a thousand birthdays, graduations, and anniversaries have been stolen from our lives by a bullet from a gun. One of those we lost was a young girl named Hadiya Pendleton. She was 15 years old. She loved Fig Newtons and lip gloss. She was a majorette. She was so good to her friends, they all thought they were her best friend. Just three weeks ago, she was here, in Washington, with her classmates, performing for her country at my inauguration. And a week later, she was shot and killed in a Chicago park after school, just a mile away from my house.[50]

Three days later he made a visit to Chicago to deliver another speech, this time to young people at Hyde Park High School. The "speech's existence" is, for some, "a victory for young people of color from Chicago and proof that Obama will respond to the voices of marginalized Americans."[51] But, on the one hand, President Obama went to Chicago because he was called there, yet he did not go to Chicago specifically to address Black Chicagoans about their concerns about their lives and the epidemic of violence there. He went there as part of the State of the Union tour, and when he arrived at Hyde Park Academy to deliver his speech, he didn't talk about love or tears or all of America sending messages of hope and healing, as he had done in Newtown. He did not center his address on the horror of the deaths of so many Black young people; he did not speak to their trauma and resilience. Instead, and unsurprisingly, the part of the speech that focused on Chicago focused on fathers and families; on marriage, morals, and hard work; on "integrity and responsibility, and discipline and delayed gratification."[52]

Put another way, when Obama spoke in Chicago at Hyde Park Academy he activated the orthography of the wake. His much-heralded speech writing seemed to suffer from dysgraphia: the inability of language to cohere around the bodies and the suffering of those who Black people who live and die in the wake and whose everyday acts insist Black life into the wake. In that February 15, 2013, speech the language of "we" and of an obligation to expend every effort to try and save every child/any child became unsustainable. As he talked about his years working with communities on the South Side Obama said:

> And those of you who worked with me, Reverend Love, you remember, it wasn't easy. Progress didn't come quickly. Sometimes I got so discouraged I thought about just giving up. But what kept me going was the belief that with enough determination and effort and persistence and perseverance, change is always possible; that *we may not* be able to help everybody, but if we help a few then that propels progress forward. *We may not* be able to save every child from gun violence, but if we save a few, that starts changing the atmosphere in our communities. [Applause.] *We may not* be able to get everybody a job right away, but if we get a few folks a job, then everybody starts feeling a little more hopeful and a little more encouraged. [Applause.] Neighborhood by neighborhood, one block by one block, one family at a time. *We may not* be able to save every child from gun violence, but if we save a few, that starts changing the atmosphere in our communities. If we

gather together what works, we can extend more ladders of opportunity for anybody who's working to build a strong, middle-class life for themselves. Because in America, your destiny shouldn't be determined by where you live, where you were born. It should be determined by how big you're willing to dream, how much effort and sweat and tears you're willing to put in to realizing that dream. (Emphasis mine)[53]

He is locked into that violent arithmetic, in which blackness disrupts the figure of the child. That dysgraphia is at work here, and so all of Obama's exhortations in Chicago and elsewhere are for us, Black people, to become Human. The hold is what is taken as a given; it is the logic; it is the characterization of relation in that moment. Obama has succumbed to the logic of the hold. I am, we are, held and held. *Wake; in the line of recoil of (a gun).*

Obama's "moral agency" was one that was willing to accept a calculus that required Black death—and that depends, to quote Joy James (2013), on "the screening out of black demands." We are returned here to Hartman (2008, 6): "Black lives are still imperiled and devalued by a racial calculus and a political arithmetic that were entrenched centuries ago. This is the afterlife of slavery—skewed life chances, limited access to health and education, premature death, incarceration, impoverishment." How else to understand the litany of names unspoken by the president, the rivers of sorrow unremarked, the traumas left in the wake of the too-young Black dead: in Chicago, in Boston, in Philadelphia, in Sanford, Florida, in Atlanta, in Los Angeles, in Ferguson, Missouri, in every town and city across the United States? How else to understand 8,063 killed and over 36,000 shot and wounded, thousands more traumatized in just fifteen years, in a small area of Chicago, just a few city blocks long and wide (see Kotlowitz 2013)?

Retinal Attachment

There is a moment in Arthur Jafa's interview with Kara Walker in his film *Dreams Are Colder Than Death* when she says that her most comfortable space of making work is the occupation of a space inserted between *her* and *her skin* and as a kind of "retinal detachment." Speaking of her most productive work space, she says,

When I find myself in this schism, in this kind of mercurial space that's sort of nongendered and nonraced and constantly being sort of encroached upon . . . my skin keeps trying to stick itself back on. . . . I'm working and then I become aware of the skin and everything that comes with it and I kind of like detach, just slightly, not all the way, it's not into that space. I'm getting this image of retinal detachment or something. The skin is literally kind of pulled away and it's kind of gory and grotesque and that's where I feel like I'm at home. It's not a safe space to be, but it's one where you can kind of look at the underside of race a little bit. (Walker, my transcription)

The kind of detachment of which Walker speaks here allows for powerful forces and images to emerge from and move through her but, I think, only within a particular range. I read her work as produced out of a particular kind of barely-tethered-to-her-Black-body experience and the ways it is held. Of course, retinal detachment also hinders one's ability to see, and untreated retinal detachment can lead to blindness: the kinds of blindnesses in, for example, Walker's first large-scale public site-specific commissioned work, *A Subtlety or The Marvelous Sugar Baby an Homage to the unpaid and overworked Artisans who have refined our Sweet tastes from the cane fields to the Kitchens of the New World on the Occasion of the demolition of the Domino Sugar Refining Plant*. In an interview with *Complex* magazine and citing Sidney Mintz, Walker talks about "the medieval fashioning of sugar, called subtleties. He [Mintz] talks about the subtleties as a medieval dish that appeared on the tables of the rich. A subtlety is a *political sugar sculpture*. They were scenes rendered in sugar paste that the nobility and the guests of the king would *recognize* as something that had political or religious importance. They were eaten as a desert or in between meals; there was this beautiful, poetic gesture" (Sargent 2014).

On that question of brutality C. L. R. James is clearer. In the opening pages of *The Black Jacobins* he details some of the everyday brutalities—meaning at any point you could see these horrors taking place—of the slaveholding class. He writes, of the enslaved, that "their masters poured burning wax on their arms and hands and shoulders, emptied the boiling cane sugar over their heads, burned them alive, roasted them on slow fires, filled them with gunpowder and blew them up with a match; buried them up to the neck and smeared their heads with sugar that the flies might devour them" (C. L. R. James 1989, 12–13). Sugar as punishment; sugar as excess; sugar as pain; sugar as pleasure. In her imagining *The Subtlety* as a gift, Walker does not enlist James's reading here, in the wake.

We are, though, living in the afterlives of that brutality that is not in the past: Robert Shelton, a former Domino Factory employee and a docent for Walker's exhibition, "recalls the difficulty of the work, the ways it was hard on the body and soul. He recalls, too, "a co-worker who continued to come to the refinery in spite of being diagnosed with terminal liver cancer in the hopes of enabling his wife to receive the $20,000 death benefit available to families if workers died on the premises. He got his wish" (Raiford and Hayes 2014).

Walker's sculpture is a "gift," and "unlike the sale of a commodity, the giving of a gift tends to establish a relationship between the parties involved.* [That asterisk appears in the text, right there.] . . . Furthermore, when gifts circulate within a group, their commerce leaves a series of interconnected relationships in its wake" (Hyde 2009, 63). What kinds of relationships are established in this giving? And receiving? It depends on what is on one's retina.

Brand, too, writes about the retina and attachments in *A Map to the Door of No Return* when she says that "the door of no return (and hence the centrality of slavery) is on her retina." And, as I have written elsewhere, I read that history for Brand as written *on* her flesh, as an optic that guides her way of seeing, understanding, and accounting for her place in the world. It is, I think, for Brand, the frame that produces Black bodies as signifiers of enslavement and its excesses, and it is the ground that positions her/us to bear the burden of *that* signification, and that positions some of us to know it (see Sharpe 2012b).

I take up, again, Brand's declaration of doorways, corners, and pursuit and those lines that follow, *I am held, and held* and I think, too, of beholding ("to see or observe a thing or person, especially a remarkable or impressive one; to hold by, keep, observe, regard, look," OED *Online*). I began this section with that door(way) that is on Brand's retina. What does one behold from the doorway? What has one beheld to declare doorways?

Albert Johnson . . . falls and he has beheld his murderer. Oscar Grant

3.4 Oscar Grant's cell phone photograph of BART officer Johannes Mehserle taken moments before he died. January 1, 2009.

beheld his murderer when he was gunned down by Johannes Mehserle. There is an image that emerged in the wake of Grant's murder on New Year's Day 2011: a photo that was retrieved from his cell phone in the following days. It is a photo of his murderer (figure 3.4). It is shot from the angle of the hold—Grant is in the hold—Mehserle is policing it. Grant has apprehended him.

The logics of the slave ship and the hold instantiated Obama's re-iteration of that terrible calculus of the inability to "save every black life": an awful arithmetic, a violence of abstraction. We are positioned in the knowledge that we are living in the afterlives of slavery, sitting in the room with history, in a lived and undeclared state of emergency. The ground of compromise, the firmament, the access to freedom and democracy, littered with Black bodies. With the optic of the door of no return on our retina, we might envision, imagine, something else—something like what Joy James (2013) calls "a liberated zone" even though under siege. Across time and space the languages and apparatus of the hold and its violences multiply; so, too, the languages of behold-ing. In what ways might we enact a beholden-ness to each other, later-ally? "Beholden: to hold by some tie of duty or obligation, to retain as a client or person in duty bound" (*OED Online*). This is what Spillers calls the intramural. How are we beholden to and beholders of each other in ways that change across time and place and space and yet remain? Beholden in the wake, as, at the very least, if we are lucky, an *opportunity* (back to the door) in our Black bodies to try to look, try to see.[54]

FOUR

The Weather

Weather: The condition of the atmosphere (at a given place and time) with respect to heat or cold, quantity of sunshine, presence or absence of rain, hail, snow, thunder, fog, etc., violence or gentleness of the winds. Also, the condition of the atmosphere regarded as subject to vicissitudes. *fig.* and in figurative context; *spec.* (*lit.*), applied to an intellectual climate, state of mind, etc. *Naut.* Of a ship, to make good, bad, etc. weather of it: to behave well or ill in a storm. Weather is described by variable conditions such as temperature, humidity, wind velocity, precipitation, and barometric pressure.

—OED *Online*

In all kinds of weather, the ships came and went from Saint Louis, Bristol, Rhode Island, New York, from Senegambia and offshore Atlantic, from West Central Africa and St. Helena, from Southeast Africa and Indian Ocean islands, from the Bight of Benin, from the Bight of Biafra, from Liverpool and Lisbon, from Bahia, Havana, Marseilles, Amsterdam, Port Antonio, Kingston, Rio de Janeiro, and London. The ships set out one in the wake of another. Five hundred years of voyages of theft, pillage, and bondage. Some of the ships made only one trip; others made multiple trips under the same and different names, under the same and different owners, and under the same and different flags, under the same and different insurers. The ships kept going and coming, over thirty-five thousand recorded voyages. I find their names in the TransAtlantic Slave Trade Voyages Database: *Antelope,*

Formiga, The Good Jesus, Diligente, Black Joke, Bonfirm, Mercúrio, The Phillis, Alligator, Voador, Tibério, The Amistad, Africa, Africain, Africaine, African Gally, Africano Constitucional, Africano Oriental, African Queen, Legítimo Africano, Vigilante Africano, Agreeable, Agreement, Aleluia da Ressurreição e Almas, the names went on and on.[1]

There were rebellions on board many of those slave ships. Other ships were intercepted or claimed at sea or in port by one jurisdiction or another. One such ship was the *Antelope,* about which it was recorded that the "original goal"—delivering the 259 surviving abducted Africans on board, 64 percent of whom were children, to the port where they would be sold—was "thwarted"; "reason human agency."[2] From Morrison's *Beloved* I draw a connection between Sethe's mother and her shipmates who made that Middle Passage crossing and that ship the *Antelope.* The figure of the *Antelope* first appears in *Beloved* through the dance that, from a distance, Sethe sees her mother and her mother's shipmates dance. As the figure appears here, I read it as it stands in for the Middle Passage and more, for other suspensions of Black being between life and death and resistance to those violent suspensions. The antelope as African cosmology and slave ship haunts the novel and repeats in the description of the fetus that Sethe is carrying as she breaks for something like freedom across the Ohio River away from the Kentucky plantation called Sweet Home. After Schoolteacher attempts to make that (left side human; right side animal) ledger flesh, Sethe breaks for supposedly free soil, carrying with her memories of another flight for freedom. "She waited for the little antelope to protest, and why she thought of an antelope Sethe could not imagine since she had never seen one. She guessed it must have been an invention held on to from before Sweet Home, when she was very young. Of that place where she was born (Carolina maybe? or was it Louisiana?) she remembered only song and dance" (Morrison 1987, 30). The text continues, "Oh but when they sang. And oh but when they danced and sometimes they danced the antelope. The men as well as the ma'ams, one of whom was certainly her own. They shifted shapes and became something other. Some unchained, demanding other whose feet knew her pulse better than she did. Just like this one in her stomach" (Morrison 1987, 31). The *Antelope* and those other ships and what occurred before them, on them, and in their wake repeat in Morrison's text and they are Weather. They haunt as Sethe gives birth to Denver in a "wrecked and wretched boat" on which she hopes to cross the Ohio River.

In *Beloved*, the weather comes, breaks, changes quickly; it "let[s] loss," it is remarked upon and forgotten; it is. In my text, the weather is the totality of our environments; the weather is the total climate; and that climate is antiblack. And while the air of freedom might linger around the ship, it does not reach into the hold, or attend the bodies in the hold. Recall Margaret Garner, on whom Morrison's Sethe is based. Margaret Garner, who first breathes Ohio's "air of freedom" when she is seven years old[3] and who, twelve years later, on the evening of January 27, 1856, escapes from Kentucky and heads back to Ohio. She has with her her four children, her husband Robert, and his parents, Mary and Simon. Of course, six years after the passage of the Fugitive Slave Act that "free air" of a "free state" is denied to those in the hold who would take their freedom; slavery is enforced as the law of the entire United States. Its atmospheric density increased; slavery undeniably became the total environment.

> By and by all trace is gone, and what is forgotten is not only the footprints but the water too and what is down there. The rest is weather. . . . Just weather. (Morrison 1987, 275)

Remember that Margaret Garner is recaptured, and in her attempt to deny ownership to those who would claim her and her children as property, she succeeds in killing her daughter Mary. After which she is recaptured, held, tried, and put on the *Henry Lewis*, that ship that will return her slavery, this time to New Orleans, a place from which almost no enslaved people managed to escape. Margaret Garner marked for that ship, stowed on it with her husband and her baby daughter, Cilla.

As the *Henry Lewis* set out on its trip to Gaines' Landing in Arkansas, it collided with the boat the *Edward Howard*. Margaret and Cilla Garner were thrown or jumped overboard. Twenty-five people died in that accident, and the Garners' infant daughter Cilla was among them. Cilla was the nursing daughter whom Garner had tried unsuccessfully to kill in order to prevent her re-abduction into slavery. When *The Liberator* and the *Cincinnati Daily Commercial* covered this, they did not report on the weather, or on the speed of the boats or on the traffic on the sometimes-crowded river. The papers reported that there was a collision and that it caused Cilla's death. The papers reported "Margaret Garner's expression of joy" on learning that the journey by ship had succeeded in killing Cilla where she had not. Another one of her children would be spared the hell of slavery (Reinhardt 2010). The papers reported that "a black man, the cook on the Lewis, sprang into the river and saved Margaret whom it was said displayed frantic joy when told that her child was drowned, and said she would never reach alive Gaines' Landing in Arkansas, the point to which she was shipped— thus indicating her intention to drown herself. . . . Another report is, that, as soon as she had an opportunity, she threw her child into the river and jumped after it. . . . It is only certain that she was in the river with her child and that it was drowned" (Reinhardt 2010, 134). The only certainties are the river, that weather (antiblackness as total climate), and that Cilla, "it" as the newspapers mis/name her, was drowned. (That oceanic ungendering repeats.)

In the wake, the river, the weather, and the drowning are death, disaster, and possibility. They are some of the impossible possibilities faced by those Black people who appear in the door and dwell in the wake. Here is Edwidge Danticat (1996b) on this: "The past is full of examples when our foremothers and forefathers showed such deep trust in the sea that they would jump off slave ships and let the waves embrace them. They too believed that the sea was the beginning and the end of all things, the road to freedom and their entrance to Guinin."

It is some of these impossible possibilities that, in *Beloved*, Sethe wants to keep from her daughter Denver. She wants to keep Denver from standing in the place where it was and is and will be; she wants to keep her from being overtaken by the past that is not past. Sethe wants to protect Denver from memory and from more than memory, from the experience, made material, of people and places that now circulate, like weather. What Sethe describes is the afterlife of slavery, and it is a "thought picture" that is out there "waiting for you." As Sethe tells Denver, memories reanimate the places and spaces of slavery post nominative emancipation. Rememory is Sethe's word for it, and it is out there, waiting for you: "What I remember," she says, "is a picture floating around out there outside my head" (Morrison 1987, 36). What Sethe remembers, rememories, and encounters in the now is the weather of being in the wake. It is weather, and even if the country, every country, any country, tries to forget and even if "every tree and grass blade of [the place] dies," it is the atmosphere: slave law transformed into lynch law, into Jim and Jane Crow, and other administrative logics that remember the brutal conditions of enslavement after the event of slavery has supposedly come to an end (Morrison 1987, 36).

In the United States, slavery is imagined as a singular event even as it changed over time and even as its duration expands into supposed emancipation and beyond. But slavery was not singular; it was, rather, a singularity—a weather event or phenomenon likely to occur around a particular time, or date, or set of circumstances. Emancipation did not make free Black life free; it continues to hold us in that singularity. The brutality was not singular; it was the singularity of antiblackness.

Singularity: a point or region of infinite mass density at which space and time are infinitely distorted by gravitational forces and which is held to be the final state of matter falling into a black hole. (Merriam-Webster Online)

In what I am calling the weather, antiblackness is pervasive *as* climate. The weather necessitates changeability and improvisation; it is the atmospheric condition of time and place; it produces new ecologies. *Ecology: the branch of biology that deals with the relations of organisms to one another and to their physical surroundings; the political movement that seeks to protect the environment, especially from pollution.* We read in *Beloved* one ecology of the ship that continues into the present: "In the beginning the women are away from the men and the men are away from the women storms rock us and mix the men into the women and the women into the men" (Morrison 1987, 211). The weather trans*forms Black being. But the shipped, the held, and those in the wake also produce out of the weather their own ecologies. When the only certainty is the weather that produces a pervasive climate of antiblackness, what must we know in order to move through these environments in which the push is always toward Black death?

An example of knowledge to survive such lived and produced ecologies comes to us via Dionne Brand's "Ruttier for the Marooned in the Diaspora." "The oral ruttier," she writes, "is a long poem containing navigational instructions which sailors learned by heart and recited from memory." The "Ruttier" (historical and present) "contained the routes and tides, the stars and maybe the taste and flavour of the waters, the coolness, the saltiness; all for finding one's way at sea" (Brand 2001, 212). Coming at the end of *A Map to the Door of No Return*, Brand's "Ruttier" has taken note of the weather, and this poem appears as a way-making tool, a gift of knowledge that, and how, Black life is lived in the wake. The inhabitants of Diaspora are

> marooned, tenantless, deserted. Desolation castaway, abandoned in the world. They was, is, wandered, wanders as spirits who dead cut, banished, seclude, refuse, shut the door, derelict, relinquished, apart. More words she has left them. Cast behind. . . . All unavailable to themselves, open to the world, cut in air. . . . And it doesn't matter where in the world, this spirit is no citizen, no national, no one who is christened, no sex, this spirit is washed of all its lading, bag and baggage, jhaji bundle, georgie bindle, lock stock, knapsack, and barrel, and only holds its own weight which is nothing, which is memoryless and tough with remembrances, heavy with lightness, aching with grins. (Brand 2001, 213)

A long poem for those of us in the wake of those ships, Brand's "Ruttier" does not contain conventional navigational instructions to country and safe landing (could it? those of us in the wake cannot use such conventional means); it does contain what present/future migrants might meet, refuse, and remake on and in their journeys. The "Ruttier" takes as ground that first plunge into unbelonging, reframes as gift that absence of country. I read the "Ruttier," then, as a way-making tool and a refusal of nation, country, citizenship; it is a barometer, a reading of and a response to those atmospheric pressures and the predictably unpredictable changes in climates that, nonetheless, remain antiblack.

The boats set out in all kinds of weather from Zliten and Tripoli and other points along the coast of Libya. These boats have no names, though they might come to be called *Left-to-Die*. Those Africans from other countries who had been living and working in Libya set out, now, because of the war, the ongoing destruction of Libya, and all that has occurred since. The atmosphere radically changed, specifically in relation to "Black Africans," and so they boarded those "wrecked and wretched boats."

"The Libyans who got me to Italy are not human," he said. "They speak with the gun not with words. . . . They pushed eight Nigerians into the sea." . . . And they pushed my friend into the sea. They all drowned.[4]

Teenagers arriving in the Italian port of Lampedusa told workers from Save the Children how migrants from sub-Saharan African countries were often kept below the deck, deprived of water and sunlight. . . . The weather was really bad. Some people were afraid. They didn't want to go, but there was no way back. (Dearden 2015)

The boats set out one after another.

And when the migrants reach the shore they are often returned to the hold in the form of the camp, the *Lager*, the detention center, and so on, and they may be returned to the ship. Cast behind, set adrift, once again.

Aspiration

> We were the offspring of lovers convicts the poor and had been
> brought to this forest by the Factory Committee
> from we born
> or. in some cases. from infancy. Many of us were mad
> some were idiots and a few suffered from enhystamines hys
> -terias vitamin deficiencies & allergies that behave like liars
> tubers & blood pressure/diseases . result of the vicious in
> -ternal breeding of our impenitential ancestors.
> —Kamau Brathwaite, The Black Angel/DS (2): Dream Stories

> We revolt simply because . . . we can no longer breathe.
> —Frantz Fanon, *Toward the African Revolution*

Again, when NourbeSe Philip asks in the Notanda to *Zong!* "What is the word for bringing bodies back from water? From a 'liquid grave'?" (Philip 2008, 202), the word she arrives at is *exaqua*. And so we ask yet again: What would it mean to stay safe and to defend the dead—our "impenitential ancestors"; those who are actually dead and those whom the state refuses to grant life; those whom the state persists in choking the life out of? I've been thinking a lot about aspiration. Not in the conventional sense. Or at least not in the sense that may most readily come to mind in which aspiration is tied to *opportunity*—that connection to the door of no return and the ship and the shipping is never far away— and tied to class movement. Tied as well, in the United States to some articulation of that deadly *occlusion* that is continually reanimated and called the American Dream. (This American Dream stands counter-poised to the dream of and in Brathwaite's *Dream Stories* and "Dream Haiti." To dream Haiti is an entirely different enterprise all together. It is to enter and inhabit the dream and reality of revolution.) I've been thinking about what it takes, in the midst of the singularity, the virulent antiblackness everywhere and always remotivated, to keep breath in the Black body. What ruttier, internalized, is necessary now to do what I am calling wake work as aspiration, that keeping breath in the Black body? I've been thinking aspiration in the complementary senses of the word: the withdrawal of fluid from the body *and* the taking in of foreign matter (usually fluid) into the lungs with the respiratory current, *and* as *audible breath* that accompanies or comprises a speech sound. Aspi-ration here, doubles, trebles in the same way that with the addition of an exclamation point, Philip transforms and breaks *Zong* from a proper name into *Zong!* That exclamation point breaks the word into song/ moan/chant/shout/breath.

It is to the breath that I want to turn now. To the necessity of breath, to breathing space, to the breathtaking spaces in the wake in which we live; and to the ways we respond, "with wonder and admiration, you are still alive, like hydrogen, like oxygen" (Brand 2015). As Philip says, the pause in the poem, the breath, "is totally subversive in the face of the kind of broad-brush brutalizing where people just get reduced to Negro man, Negro woman, and ditto, ditto, ditto. You pay attention to one, and it is such an amazing act—and one that spills over to all the other dit-tos—paying attention and taking care with just the one. Because that's all we can do is care one by one by one. And that's why it was so impor-tant for me to name these lost souls in the footnotes to the early poems" (Saunders 2008a, 78). Breathlessness and the archive: the archives of breathlessness. The details accumulate in *Zong!* and for us, what might it mean to attend to these archives? What might we discover in them?

In 1982, Los Angeles police chief Daryl Gates "provoked an outcry from civil rights advocates when he said that blacks might be more likely to die from choke holds because their arteries do not open as fast as arteries do on 'normal people.'"[5] Nine years later, but only seven months after the March 3, 1991, beating-almost-to-death of Rodney King in which we marveled that he was still alive (*"like hydrogen, like oxygen"*), "some Police Department tactical experts now see the videotape of officers striking Mr. King 56 times as an opportunity to convince the public the choke hold is actually safer and a more humane way to subdue suspects."[6] In New York City, though police chokeholds were banned for over two decades, "the Civilian Complaint Review Board has seen 1,128 chokehold cases over the last five-and-a-half years, and complaints about the practice 'persist and appear to be increasing.'"[7]

"I can't breathe." On July 17, 2014, Eric Garner was on the street in Staten Island when he was approached and stopped by an NYPD officer "on suspicion of selling loose, untaxed cigarettes." Mr. Garner is (and I am reading/hearing echoes of Margaret Garner in all of this) approached by the NYPD, and he responds to the stop by saying, "For what? Every time you see me you want to mess with me. I'm tired of it. This stops today. What are you bothering me for. . . . I didn't do nothing. . . . I'm just standing here. I did not sell nothing. Because every time you see me, you want to stop me, you harass me. . . . I'm minding my business, officer. I'm minding my business; please just leave me alone. I told you the last time, please just leave me alone."[8] Then two other officers approach Mr. Garner and he repeats his pleas not to be touched: "Don't touch me, don't touch me, please." And then the first officer, Pantaleo, puts Mr. Garner in a chokehold and takes him down to the ground. Eleven times during this assault Mr. Garner says, "I can't breathe, I can't breathe, I can't breathe, I can't breathe, I can't breathe, I can't breathe, I can't breathe, I can't breathe, I can't breathe, I can't breathe, I can't breathe" until he stops breathing. And though paramedics have arrived on the scene, they give him no assistance. No aspiration. The city medical examiner ruled Mr. Garner's death a homicide, and despite audio and visual evidence, the NYPD maintains its claim that the cause of this murder (for which they will find no one, save Mr. Garner, responsible) was *not* a chokehold, and once again, Mr. Garner's murderer was not indicted. The list of nonindictments in the wake of state murders of Black people continues to grow: Michael Brown, John Crawford, Aiyana Stanley-Jones, Sandra Bland, Jonathan Ferrell, Miriam Carey, Tamir Rice, Rekia Boyd, *. Again, Black being appears in the space of the asterisked human as the insurance for, as that which underwrites, white circulation as the human. Always, Black being seems lodged between cargo and being. *Wake: in the line of recoil of (a gun). Wake: the track left on the water's surface by a ship. Wake: the watching of relatives and friends beside the body of the dead person.*

It was soon after Eric Garner's murder on July 17, 2014, that the jury in the trial of Ted Wafer returned a verdict of guilty in the case of his murder of nineteen-year-old Renisha McBride.[9] The previous July had seen the all-(non Black)woman jury return a verdict of not guilty for George Zimmerman, the murderer of seventeen-year-old Trayvon Martin.[10] The verdict in the Wafer trial brought, perhaps, a little breathing room before the next onslaught, the next intake of air, the held breath. In the weather of the wake, one cannot trust, support, or condone the state's application of something they call justice, but one can only hold one's breath for so long. "*'We revolt simply because, for a variety of reasons, we can no longer breathe'*" (Fanon [1970] 1994, 50).

Day after day the stories arrive. Fifty people suffocated in the hold of a ship;[11] three people suffocated in prison over the course of a weekend in the United States. To explicate Fanon, it is not the specifics of any one event or set of events that are endlessly repeatable and repeated, but the totality of the environments in which we struggle; the machines in which we live; what I am calling the weather.

In an interview in the *Atlantic* about *Breathing Race into the Machine*, her book on racial science and the invention and use of the spirometer, the instrument that measures lung capacity, Lundy Braun says,

> In 1864, the year before the Civil War ended, a massive study was launched to quantify the bodies of Union soldiers. One key finding in what would become a 613-page report was that soldiers classified as "White" had a higher lung capacity than those labeled "Full Blacks" or "Mulattoes." The study relied on the spirometer—a medical instrument that measures lung capacity. This device was previously used by plantation physicians to show that black slaves had weaker lungs than white citizens. The Civil War study seemed to validate this view. As early as Thomas Jefferson's *Notes on the State of Virginia*, in which he remarked on the dysfunction of the "pulmonary apparatus" of blacks, lungs were used as a marker of difference, a sign that black bodies were fit for the field and little else. (Forced labor was seen as a way to "vitalize the blood" of flawed black physiology. By this logic, slavery is what kept black bodies alive.) (Braun and Shaban 2014)

Daryl Gates and contemporary policing practices are the inheritors of the history of the spirometer that produced Black bodies as defective and monstrous.

There is, too, a connection between the lungs and the weather: the supposedly transformative properties of breathing free air—that which throws off the mantle of slavery—and the transformative properties of being "free" to breathe fresh air. These discourses run through freedom narratives habitually. But who has access to freedom? Who can breathe free? Those narratives do not ameliorate this lack; this lack is the atmosphere of antiblackness. Recall, too, that captive Africans were brought out of the hold, weather permitting, to put fresh air in their lungs and to be exercised. (Of course, this was about their value as cargo and not about the health of the captive Africans for themselves. This is being, property, for the other.) Weather monitoring was a major part of plantation management. Awareness of the ecological systems was necessary for the growth and cultivation of certain crops (growing seasons, yield, etc.) and for the life expectancy (or lack of) of the captive laboring population. We read, "Planters consistently recorded the weather in their work logs as part of the revolution in plantation accounting techniques" (Roberts 2013, 195). Weather determined local practices of working enslaved people, and those practices differed from plantation to plantation and from region to region. Some slave owners believed in working enslaved people harder in the rain, while under the same conditions other slave owners assigned the enslaved "lighter" tasks. Overall, though, enslaved people had very little respite from work even when plantation managers believed that work in the rain produced a miasma or "bad air." One Jamaican planter reports "not a single day of work lost to weather over the course of two years" (Roberts 2013, 196). Regardless of the particular practices, relentless hard labor in the rain, in the sun, in damp and in dry, cutting cane, laying dung, hoeing, and weeding, all had deleterious and often deadly effects on the lungs and bodies of the enslaved.

Slavery, then, simultaneously exhausted the lungs and bodies of the enslaved even as it was imagined and operationalized as that which kept breath in and vitalized the Black body. We, now, are living in the wake of such pseudoscience, living the time when our labor is no longer necessary but our flesh, our bodies, are still the stuff out of which "democracy" is produced. Back to Fanon ([1970]1994, 50), who wrote in *Toward the African Revolution,* "There is not occupation of territory, on the one hand, and independence of persons on the other. It is the country as a whole, its history, its daily pulsation that are contested, disfigured . . . under these conditions; the individual's breathing is an observed breathing. It is a combat breathing."

What is the word for keeping and putting breath back in the body? What is the word for how we must approach the archives of slavery (to "tell the story that cannot be told") and the histories and presents of violent extraction *in* slavery *and* incarceration; the calamities and catastrophes that sometimes answer to the names of occupation, colonialism, imperialism, tourism, militarism, or humanitarian aid and intervention? What are the words and forms for the ways we must continue to think and imagine laterally, across a series of relations in the hold, in multiple Black everydays of the wake? The word that I arrived at for such imagining and for keeping and putting breath back in the Black body in hostile weather is *aspiration* (and aspiration is violent and lifesaving). Two additional forms of wake work as a praxis for imagining, arrive in the registers of Black annotation and Black redaction.

Black Annotation, Black Redaction

Annotate: To add notes to, furnish with notes (a literary work or author).
An annotation is metadata (e.g. a comment, explanation, presentational markup) attached to text, image, or other data. Often annotations refer to a specific part of the original data.
—OED *Online*

Redaction: a: The action of bringing or putting into a definite form; (now) *spec.* the working or drafting of source material into a distinct, esp. written, form. Usu. with *into,* (occas.) *to.*
b: The action or process of revising or editing text, esp. in preparation for publication; (also) an act of editorial revision.
Obs. The action of driving back; resistance, reaction.
—OED *Online*

I point to these practices of Black annotation and Black redaction as more examples of wake work. The orthographies of the wake require new modes of writing, new modes of making-sensible. Redaction comes to us most familiarly through those blacked-out "sensitive

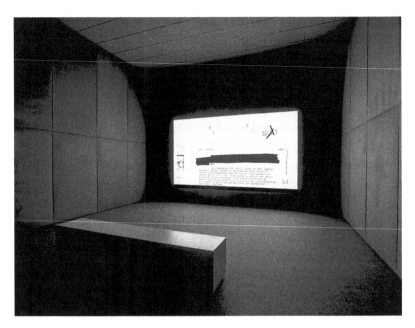

4.1 Steve McQueen, *End Credits*, 2012. Sequence of digitally scanned files, sound, continuous projection. Installation at the Art Institute, Chicago, 2013. Courtesy of the artist; Marian Goodman Gallery and Thomas Dane Gallery, London

lines" in certain government documents that contain information we are not allowed to read. Steve McQueen's film *End Credits* (2012) consists of six hours of images and voiceover of the redacted FBI files of Paul Robeson. As I watched and listened, it again became clear to me that so much of Black intramural life and social and political work is redacted, made invisible to the present and future, subtended by plantation logics, detached optics, and brutal architectures.

There is, in the Black diaspora (and I include the Continent here because of colonial histories and presents and trans*migration) a long history of Black life, of Black lives being annotated and redacted. There is, as well, continuous resistance to and disruption of those violent annotations and redactions. A 2015 conference on Black portraiture has the subtitle *Imaging the Body and Re-Staging Histories*. Each time I read that word *imaging* I read it doubly. That is, I read the word as *imaging*, "to make a representation of the external form of," and also as *imagining*, "to form a mental image or concept of; to suppose or assume; the ability to form mental images of things that either are not physically present or have never been conceived or created by others."[12] If we understand portraiture to be both the "art of creating portraits" (image and text) and "graphic and detailed description," how might we understand a variety of forms of contemporary Black public image-making in and as refusals to accede to the optics, the disciplines, and the deathly demands of the antiblack worlds in which we live, work, and struggle to make visible (to ourselves, if not to others) all kinds of Black pasts, presents, and possible futures? Much of the work of Black imaging and the work that those images do out in the world has been about such imaginings of the fullness of Black life. In *Cutting a Figure: Fashioning Black Portraiture*, Richard Powell (2008, xv) writes that "a significant segment of black portraiture stands apart from the rest of the genre, and not only because of the historical and social realities of racism. Rather, the difference often lies in the artistic contract between the portrayer and portrayed; conscious or unconscious negotiations that invest black subjects with social capital." While Powell speaks here of Black artists and subjects' negotiated and reciprocal imaginings, I want to think about those portraits outside of our own imaging and imagining in which, to borrow from Huey Copeland (2013), we seem "bound to appear." There is a long history and present of resistance to, disruption and refashioning of images of blackness and Black people. There is a long history and present of imaging and imagining black-ness and Black selves otherwise, in excess of the containment of the long and brutal history of the violent annotations of Black being: what Spillers, for example, called the hieroglyphics of the flesh; a history that is "the crisis of referentiality, the fictions of personhood, and the gap or incommensurability between the proper name and the form of existence that it signifies" (Hartman 2014). I am thinking here, ushering here, into the gap, Black annotation together with Black redaction, not as opposites, but as trans*verse *and* coextensive ways to imagine otherwise.

Put another way, I want to think annotation in relation to the dys-graphia and the orthography of the wake; in relation to those photo-graphs of Black people in distress that appear so regularly in our lives, whether the image of that suffering Black person comes from quotidian or extraordinary disasters, the photos of them often hit in the regis-ter of abandonment. The photographs do this even, or even especially, when they purport to "humanize" Black people—that is, they purport to make *manifest* "humanity" that we already know to be present.[13] To be clear, just as I am not interested in rescuing the term *girl* (see "The Ship"), I am not interested in rescuing Black being(s) for the category of the "Human," misunderstood as "Man," or for the languages of development. Both of those languages and the material conditions that they re/produce continue to produce our fast and slow deaths. I am interested in ways of seeing and imagining responses to the terror visited on Black life and the ways we inhabit it, are inhabited by it, and refuse it. I am interested in the ways we live in and despite that terror. By considering that relationship between imaging and imagining in the registers of Black annotation and Black redaction, I want to think about what these images call forth. And I want to think through what they call on us to do, think, feel in the wake of slavery—which is to say, in an ongoing present of subjection and resistance.

Annotation appears like that asterisk, which is itself an annotation mark, that marks the trans*formation into ontological blackness. As photographs of Black people circulate as portraits in a variety of publics, they are often accompanied by some sort of note or other metadata, whether that notation is in the photograph itself or as a response to a dehumaning photograph, in order that the image might travel with supplemental information that marks injury and, then, more than injury. We know that, as far as images of Black people are concerned, in their circulation they often don't, in fact, do the imaging work that we expect of them. There are too many examples of this to name: from the videotaped beating of Rodney King in 1991, to the murder of Oscar Grant, to the brutal murders of twenty-one trans women in the United States as of November 2015, to all of the circulating images of and in the aftermath of Hurricane Katrina and the 2010 earthquake in Haiti, to the ongoing deaths in transatlantic, trans-Mediterranean, and transcontinental crossings extending across the Black global diaspora. This is true even though and when we find images of Black suffering in various publics framed in and as calls to action or calls to feel with and for. Most often these images function as a hail to the non Black person in the Althusserian sense. That is, these images work to confirm the status, location, and already held opinions within dominant ideology about those exhibitions of spectacular Black bodies whose meanings then remain unchanged. We have been reminded by Hartman and many others that the repetition of the visual, discursive, state, and other quotidian and extraordinary cruel and unusual violences enacted on Black people does not lead to a cessation of violence, nor does it, across or within communities, lead primarily to sympathy or something like empathy. Such repetitions often work to solidify and make continuous the colonial project of violence. With that knowledge in mind, what kinds of ethical viewing and reading practices must we employ, *now*, in the face of these onslaughts? What might practices of Black annotation and Black redaction offer?

What follows are three examples of what I am calling Black visual/textual annotation and redaction. Redaction and annotation toward seeing and reading otherwise; toward reading and seeing something in excess of what is caught in the frame; toward seeing something beyond a visuality that is, as Nicholas Mirzoeff (2011) argues, subtended by the logics of the administered plantation. In "Home," Toni Morrison (1998, 7) writes that she has consistently tried "to carve away the accretions of deceit, blindness, ignorance, paralysis, and sheer malevolence embedded in raced language so that other kinds of perception were not only available but were inevitable." I am imagining that the work of Black annotation and Black redaction is to enact the movement to that inevitable — a counter to abandonment, another effort to try to look, to try to really see.[14]

I return, again, to the photograph of the little girl with the word *Ship* affixed to her forehead (figure 2.5). This little girl was at the beginning of this work, and she occupies its center. Shortly after that catastrophic earthquake hit Haiti on January 12, 2010, I entered the archive of photographs that had emerged from it. It wasn't the first time I had cautiously entered this archive, but on this occasion I was stopped by that photograph of a young Black girl, ten years old at most. A third of the image is blurry. But on the right-hand side one can still make out grass and dirt, something black that she is lying on, and, in the background, other things (a figure? a bundle of clothing? a cigarette? something else?).

The girl's face is clear; it's what's in focus. She is alive. Her eyes are open. She is lying on what looks like a black stretcher; her head is on a cold pack, and you can make out that there is writing on that cold pack and some of the words, like *instructions for use and disposal*. You can also read the words *roll up* and *dispose* and *registered trademark*. There's some debris on the stretcher. There are two uncovered wounds over the girl's right eye and another smaller one under it. A piece of paper is stuck to her bottom lip. She is wearing what seems to be a print cotton hospital gown. She is looking straight ahead of her, or directly at, or past, the photographer's camera. She looks to be in shock. Her big black eyes, with their lush eyelashes, look glazed. Her look reaches out to me. Affixed to her forehead is that piece of transparent tape with the word *Ship* written on it. What is the look in her eyes? What do I do with it? The first annotation was that word *Ship*. What can one see beyond that word that threatens to block out everything else?

When I stumbled upon that image of this girl child with the word *Ship* taped to her forehead, it was the look in her eyes that stopped me. Then with its coming into focus that word *Ship* threatened to obliterate everything and anything else I could see. What was it doing there, I wondered? But I returned again and again to that photo and to her face to ask myself about the look in her eyes. What was I being called to by and with her look at me and mine at her? Over the course of the years since I first found that image of this girl, I returned to it repeatedly to try to account for what I saw or thought I might see. Where is she looking? Who and what is she looking at or looking for? Who can look back? Does she know that there is a piece of tape on her forehead? Does she know what that piece of tape says? She must be afraid. Does she know that she is already linked to a ship and that she is destined for yet another one? Her eyes look back at me, like Delia's eyes, like Drana's.[15]

In a move that is counter to the way photographic redaction usually works—where the eyes are covered and the rest of the face remains visible—here I include only Delia's and Drana's eyes. I performed my own redaction of Agassiz's ethnographic images in order to focus in on their eyes. I redact the images to focus their individual and collective looks out and past the white people who claimed power over them and the instrument by which they are being further subjected in ways they could never have imagined or anticipated. I want to see *their* looks out and past and across time. Delia and Drana. In my look at them, I register in their eyes an "I" and a "we" that is and are holding something in, holding on, and held, still. Delia and Drana sitting there (still) and then standing there (still), and clothed and unclothed (still) and protected only by eyelashes (still).[16] I am reminded here, of the anagrammatical life of the word *still* for the enslaved and for all Black people in slavery's wake. Over the course of a paragraph in *Beloved* Morrison elaborates what *still* means for the heavily pregnant Sethe, who at this point in her

4.2 Joseph T. Zealy, Delia, country born of African parents, daughter, Renty. Congo. Delia's eyes. Detail. Courtesy of the Peabody Museum of Archaeology and Ethnology, Harvard University, PM# 35-5-1/053040 (digital file# 60742034 DETAIL)

4.3 Joseph T. Zealy, Drana, country born, daughter of Jack, Guinea, plantation of B. F. Taylor Esq. Drana's eyes. Detail. Courtesy of the Peabody Museum of Archaeology and Ethnology, Harvard University, PM #35-5-1/053041 (digital file# 60742035 DETAIL)

pregnancy "was walking on two feet meant for standing still . . . still, near a kettle; still at the churn; still, at the tub and ironing board" (Morrison 1987, 29–30). I am reminded here of *still* as it repeats in Brand's *Verso 55* (2015), marked as it is there, with wonder at our survival and the residence time of the wake: "We felt pity for them, and affection and love; they felt happy for us, we were still alive. Yes, we are still alive we said. And we had returned to thank them. You are still alive, they said. Yes we are still alive. They looked at us like violet; like violet teas they drank us. We said here we are. They said, you are still alive. We said, yes, yes we are still alive." Delia and Drana, marked, still, because of the daguerreotype's long exposure time, which required that one hold still for long periods of time, and because they were of the ship yet not immediately off the ship like their fathers identified as Renty (Congo) and Jack (Guinea). The little girl who survives the 2010 Haitian earthquake is also a descendant of the ship and she is marked still, and once again, for its hold. I looked again at that photo and I marked her youth, the diagonal scar that cuts across the bridge of her nose and into her eyebrow, those extravagant eyelashes that curl back to the lid, the uncovered wounds, that bit of paper on her lip, and a leaf on the gown and in her hair. *"standing here in eyelashes, in/ . . . /the brittle gnawed life we live,/ I am held, and held."*

I marked the violence of the quake that deposited that little girl there, injured, in this archive, and the violence in the name of care of the placement of that taped word on her forehead, and then I kept looking because that could not be all there was to see or say. *I had to take care.* (A different kind of care and a different optic than the ones employed in the wake of the *Zorgue*, that ship called Care.) I was looking for more than the violence of the slave ship, the migrant and refugee ship, the container ship, and the medical ship. I saw that leaf in her hair, and with it I performed my own annotation that might open this image out into a life, however precarious, that was always there.[17] *That leaf is stuck in her still neat braids.* And I think: *Somebody braided her hair before that earthquake hit.*

The Little Girl Who Wrote "Hi"

She comes to us from the front pages of the *New York Times*, a December 10, 2014, article titled "Schools' Discipline for Girls Differs by Race and Hue" and with the caption "Mikia Hutchings, 12, whose writing on a wall at school led to a juvenile criminal case, and her lawyer, Michael J. Tafelski, waiting for a meeting held last month by a Georgia state committee studying school discipline."[18] Writing is discovered on a school gym bathroom wall. Two middle school students are accused of vandalism: Mikia Hutchings, who is Black, and her (unnamed in the article) white girlfriend. When Mikia's family is alerted to the charges against her, they find it hard to believe she was involved in defacing school and personal property. Then they report to the authorities that they cannot afford to pay the hundred-dollar "restitution" fee to the school and to the student whose sneakers were damaged. "While both students were suspended from school for a few days, Mikia had to face a school disciplinary hearing and, a few weeks later, a visit by a uniformed officer from the local Sheriff's Department, who served her grandmother with papers accusing Mikia of a trespassing misdemeanor and, potentially, a felony" (Vega 2014). Because her family is unable to pay the money, Mikia will be made to pay a much larger price. "As part of an agreement with the state to have the charges dismissed in juvenile court, Mikia admitted to the allegations of criminal trespassing. Mikia, who is African-American, spent her summer on probation, under a 7 p.m. curfew, and had to complete 16 hours of community service in addition to writing an apology letter to a student whose sneakers were defaced in the incident. *Her friend, who is white, was let go after her parents paid restitution*" (Vega 2014).

The article is sympathetic to Mikia. It tries to bring her into focus, and yet she disappears in description. The introductory paragraph reads: "To hear Mikia Hutchings speak, one must lean in close, as her voice barely rises above a whisper. In report cards, her teachers describe her as 'very focused,' someone who follows the rules and stays on task. So it was a surprise for her grandmother when Mikia, 12, and a friend got into trouble for writing graffiti on the walls of a gym bathroom at Dutchtown Middle School in Henry County last year" (Vega 2014).

See and hear Mikia Hutchings. She is a child, a young Black girl, just twelve years old and slight. In the photograph she appears, captured, her lower back resting against a wall as she leans forward, beside a classroom door. She is wearing a gray-and-black horizontal-striped shirt, black stretch pants, black boots with white turned-over cuffs, and a light blue insulated jacket with a hood and a white collar, trim, and

4.4 Mikia Hutchings, twelve, and her lawyer, Michael Tafelski, wait for a disciplinary hearing at the Henry County Board of Education building in McDonough, Georgia, November 18, 2014. Hutchings and a white friend faced very different disciplinary actions for the same minor incident of vandalism, part of what some see as bias in a state where black girls are five times more likely to be suspended from school than white ones. © Kevin Liles/The New York Times/Redux

white cuffs that echo the white cuffs on the boots. She looks down and to the side, and the fingers of her left hand hold one finger of her right hand. (She holds herself, holds onto herself.) What is the look on her face? As she appears here, she is physically overwhelmed by her white male legal representative, by the charges against her and all of the authority that has been summoned and is determined to discipline her. This authority, the police, the courts, the school, and so on, would put her in cuffs; they have been summoned to transform this girl into a felon. As it abuts the modifier Black, "girl" here, again, appears as the anagrammatical. "'When a darker-skinned African-American female acts up, there's a certain concern about their boyish aggressiveness,' Dr. Hannon said, 'that they don't know their place as a female, as a woman'" (Vega 2014). Mikia Hutchings is held, and in that holding once again "girl" is thrown into question.

If we annotate and redact that first paragraph of the *New York Times* article, we might find Mikia's point of view. Through redaction we might hear what she has to say in her own defense in the midst of the ways she is made to appear only to be made to disappear. Put another way, with our own Black annotations and Black redactions, we might locate a counter to the force of the state (care as force; "the provision of what is necessary for the health, welfare, maintenance, and protection of someone or something") that has landed her on the front page of the *New York Times*. With this analytic we might begin to see and hear Mikia, whose sole offense was writing the word "Hi" on the wall while a young, Black girl child without financial resources.

That I am arguing for Mikia to come into sight should not be mistaken as an argument for representation or representational politics.

Rather, Black annotation and Black redaction are ways to make Black life visible, if only momentarily, through the optic of the door. Black annotation and redaction meet the Black anagrammatical and the failure of words and concepts to hold in and on Black flesh. Think, now, of the annotations and redactions of the second autopsies ordered by the families of the murdered and commissioned in the wake of so many murders. The second autopsy performed on Michael Brown was requested by his family and their legal team in order to show injury. In other words, that second autopsy was ordered to show the harm done to Michael Brown, who was shot at least six times, including two times in the head. As with Lamont Adams, the bullet wounds to Michael Brown's hand suggested that he was in the posture of surrender. By securing that second autopsy, his family tried to disrupt the dysgraphia that wrote a version of events that was riven with antiblackness. It was not enough to see Michael Brown's body uncovered in the street for hours on a hot August day, his mother and stepfather prevented from going to his side. It was not enough to see his mother's distress, to see and hear her scream and fall into the arms of family members. It was not enough to see his distraught stepfather on the side of the road with a makeshift sign declaring: "The police just murdered my son." Not enough. And so his family added their own annotations; they tried to come up with his body's harms as seen through their eyes in order to contest that body that was drawn by antiblackness (figure 4.5). And, of course, even then, it is not enough. It cannot be enough. They cannot recuperate his body. The constant production of Black death *is* and *as* necessary returns us to the singularity. But just as the weather is always ripe for Black death, the singularity also produces Black resistances and refusals.

Black redaction and Black annotation are ways of imagining otherwise. I turn here to Julie Dash's *Daughters of the Dust* (1992). *Daughters* was produced over the course of ten years, and it emanated from the politics and aesthetics that began with Dash's work as part of the LA Rebellion, along with other filmmakers, like Charles Burnett and Haile Gerima. When it was released in 1992, *Daughters* became the first film by an African American woman to get cinematic distribution in the United States. It found an immediate audience with Black women, and at the same time it came to be seen by many other viewing audiences as a foreign film because it did not deal in the familiar.

It was Dash and cinematographer Arthur Jafa's aim to unmake colonial optics that occupy and reproduce the retinal detachment that, then, reproduces the hold as location and destination. That that is their aim is clear from the first shot of the film, which takes place on a boat. In that opening scene we are introduced to Viola Peazant; Mr. Snead, the photographer she has hired to document the migration of her family; her long-gone cousin Yellow Mary; and Yellow Mary's lover Trula. Mr. Snead shows Yellow Mary and Trula the kaleidoscope he has brought with him. He explains the word's etymology as "*Kalos* . . . Beautiful. *Eidos* . . . Form. *Skopein* . . . [to see]" (Dash 1992, 82). As he speaks, Yellow Mary looks at Trula through the kaleidoscope, and Viola explains to Mr. Snead that the slave trade, the importation of "fresh Africans," continued "back off these islands" for many years after it was banned (Dash 1992, 84). This scene establishes for the audience its entrance into a complex visual scene as it interrogates established knowledges:

CASE NO. _____ NAME *MICHAEL BROWN*

Entry, reentry and exit perforations, preliminary autopsy report

DIAGRAM A   *Figure 25 (17)*

M. Baden
08/19/2014

4.5 Preliminary autopsy report delineating wounds on Michael Brown's body. Courtesy of Dr. Michael M. Baden the time when slavery ended, what the archives don't record. The photographer with his optical equipment, the conversations they have on the boat, and the deliberate way the characters look at and away from each other prepare the audience for something formally beautiful and something that challenges their assumed viewing habits. The slowing down of some of the shots from twenty-four to sixteen frames per second is also a reconfiguration of ways of seeing, and in those instances when the film slows down, an additional space is created for the audience to enter into the scene. Dash (1992, 16, 25) says that she "was told over and over again that there was no market for the film. The distributors talked about the spectacular look of the film and the images and story being so different and thought-provoking, yet the consistent response was that there was 'no market' for this type of film."

With those additional spaces and with her visual and aesthetic choices for marking slavery's long time, Dash engages in some of her own Black redactions. By which I mean, her redaction is her decision to show the traces of slavery as the indigo blue that remains on the hands of the formerly enslaved people who labored and died over the poisonous indigo pits on the Sea Islands off of the coast of South Carolina. Though Dash was well aware that the indigo stains would no longer be visible forty years after the end of legal chattel slavery, she chose this image as the trace of slavery rather than whip-scarred backs, brands, or other more familiar marks that are all too visible in, for example, Steve McQueen's *Twelve Years a Slave* (2013). For Dash, the indigo is what endures as trace, and this trace positions viewers differently in relation to the fact that the afterlives of slavery are long and that the life span of the enslaved people who labored over the pits was very short. "From fifty to sixty hands work in the indigo factory; and such is the effect of the indigo upon the lungs of the laborers, that they never live over seven years. Every one that runs away, and is caught, is put in the indigo fields, which are hedged all around, so that they cannot escape again."[19]

Twelve Years a Slave is a film that McQueen has said "is about love" and that his work here, "is about keeping the tension." He continues, "I love the idea of just being in real time, being present, being there. I'm a filmmaker, so I always think: 'When is the breaking point? When is long enough?'"[20] If we think *Daughters* alongside *Twelve Years*, we might ask where and when is the breaking point in the latter film, or for that matter in most contemporary films in the West, in their representations of Black suffering (of the wake, the hold, the weather, the ship). Where is the breaking point, the breath, the pause, where the circulation, production, and reception of images of Black suffering and, importantly, the pleasure in them are concerned? The long time/ the long shot, the residence time of Black life always on the verge of and in death, goes on. As it appears in *Twelve Years a Slave* (whether in the vicious extended beating of Patsey or in the four-minute-long take of Northrup's hanging), it enters the everyday as continuous and gratuitous. Not so in *Daughters of the Dust* and its visualization of Black life in the decades after slavery's end, as one family is about to migrate from the South to the North of the United States.

Not so in Mauritanian filmmaker Abderrahmane Sissako's gorgeous film *Timbuktu* (2014), which tells a story of life lived in the immanence and imminence of death and in the midst of great violent change. *Timbuktu* makes tangible the ways life is lived in the wake and under the pressure of tremendous change. In Sissako's film the year is 2012 and the pressure is Ansar Dine's takeover of Timbuktu, Mali. They banned music; they made women cover their faces, heads, and hands; they forbade play; and they introduced strict Islamic law. Sissako visualizes life in the midst of those impositions that drastically change the lives of the people in Timbuktu. There is a group of young boys who—in the moments that they are not being watched by the men and boys with guns, some of those boys not much older than themselves—play a full and beautifully imagined and executed football match without a football because football has been banned. There is a young woman who has been caught and found guilty of the crime of making music together in a room with three friends, another woman and two men. She is sentenced to forty lashes. In the midst of this vicious public beating her weeping breaks into song. (From *Zong* [which again means "song"] to Philip's *Zong!*) This is, again, the time of the oral ruttier, and those songs help us find our way; they are our internalized maps in the long time of our displacement. *"We sing for death, we sing for birth. That's what we do. We sing."*

There is another woman who appears several times in Sissako's *Timbuktu*. Each time she appears in the film she is moving unmolested through the town and she is wearing a fantastic dress made of brightly colored strips of cloth that trail into a long indigo train. This woman refuses to cover her head or hands or face; she holds up traffic, she strolls past the men and boys with guns, she refuses to cower before them; she laughs at their commands, these men who have descended on and taken over Timbuktu, the enforcers of Islamic law who smoke in secret and have long conversations with each other about music and professional football. Of the women in the city she is not alone in her refusal; every woman in *Timbuktu* resists, but this woman alone faces no reprisal.

There is a stunning moment in the film when this fantastically dressed woman appears on screen and speaks. We learn that her name is Zabou, and when she speaks Haiti erupts into Sissako's *Timbuktu*. Zabou speaks and her words return us to Brathwaite's *Dream Haiti* and its collapse of time and space.[21] Her words return us to the dream and promise and centrality of Haiti in diaspora imaginings.

What Zabou says is this: "It was on the twelfth of January 2010 and 4:53 p.m. exactly, the same time as Miami. At 4:53 p.m., Port-au-Prince time, the earth quaked and I found myself here, at exactly 9:53 p.m." Zabou asks one of the men, drawn to Timbuktu from all over the continent, for confirmation of this. But the man replies that she was in Timbuktu long before that earthquake hit. To which Zabou retorts: "What is time?" She continues: "Time doesn't matter. The earthquake is my body, the cracks, it's me! Cracked open from head to toe and vice versa, my arms, my back and my face, cracked. What is time? I am cracked. Sweetpea, you and I are alike. We're both cracked. Cracked everywhere" (figures 4.6–4.8).

Time. In *Beloved*, time "never worked the way Sixo thought." In *Beloved*, Sethe has trouble believing in it because "some things go. Pass on. Some things just stay" (Morrison 1987, 21, 35). Time appears here as cracked. Time is cracked like Zabou's body, like Zabou's life, and not only her life. She tells the young man with a gun (who appears to have been a dancer in his former life) that he, too, is cracked. Zabou doesn't believe in time, at least not linear time. She lives in trans*Atlantic time, in an oceanic time that does not pass, a time in which the past and present verge. "Time doesn't matter," Zabou says again, and I hear in her speaking the longue durée, the residence time, of the wake.

Zabou moves through Sissako's film, trailing that long indigo train, blue like the sea, a V like a wave; like a wake; it is a crack that follows her, a crack that precedes her. Sissako has opened a seam in Timbuktu and inserted Haiti; Sissako has opened a seam in Timbuktu, and from

4.6–4.8 Film stills. *Timbuktu*. © 2014 Les films du Worso — Dune
Vision — Arches Films — ARTE France Cinéma — Orange Studio.
With the courtesy of LE PACTE

it Haiti has emerged. Zabou's blue train, like the indigo on the hands of the formerly enslaved in *Daughters of the Dust*, like the violet teas and the violet chemistry of Brand's *Verso 55*, like water, like the ruptures of the transatlantic and trans-Arab slave trades, appears and opens the film into and out of all of the violences and more, as so many aftershocks, as so many wakes. The work that *Daughters* and *Timbuktu* perform is wake work.

And in Zabou's speech I hear a connection to what Beverly Bell describes in *Fault Lines: Views across Haiti's Divide* in the aftermath of the earthquake. Writing about the work that began in Haiti as soon as the first tremors stopped, and of the poor who had to continue to live in the midst of ongoing destruction, Bell (2013, 3) says: "They knew that their country's devastation—before the earthquake as now—was not inevitable." The work that I am theorizing as wake work took place in Haiti in the midst of searching for the injured, mourning the dead and dying, and sitting with those who hovered on the brink between material life and death. This was work that Haitian people knew would have to be done, and in carrying it out they drew on the "alternative principles and practices that the grassroots have tried to establish over time" (Bell 2013, 4). There is a before and an after to the earthquake: but there is no before the ongoing event of the disaster.[22] How, after all, to split time?

I hear in Zabou's outrage an echo of the outrage in novelist Fatou Diome's interview. I repeat, here, the words from Diome that began this section: "These people whose bodies are washing up on these shores,— and I carefully choose my words—if they were Whites, the whole Earth should be shaking now."[23] I hear an echo of Danticat (1996b) capturing the insistence with which Haitian women speak themselves into the present. Their greeting: "How are we today, Sister?/I am ugly, but I am here."

Coda

Aspiration. *Aspiration* is the word that I arrived at for keeping and putting breath in the Black body.

Living as I have argued we do in the wake of slavery, in spaces where we were never meant to survive, or have been punished for surviving and for daring to claim or make spaces of something like freedom, we yet reimagine and transform spaces for and practices of an ethics of care (as in repair, maintenance, attention), an ethics of seeing, and of *being* in the wake as consciousness; as a way of remembering and observance that started with the door of no return, continued in the hold of the ship and on the shore. As one survivor of the contemporary ship and the hold says, "We couldn't put him in the middle of the boat because the boat was damaged and we were taking on water. If we left him like this, he'd be gone, whoosh. So, we were really careful with him. I like things like this—when people care. It's all we have."[24] This is an account counter to the violence of abstraction, an account of surviving the ship when the wake, the ship, the hold, and the weather and their un/survival repeat and repeat. An account of *care* as shared risk between and among the Black trans*asterisked.

Dionne Brand offers us such accounts of care in all of her work. She moves in *A Map to the Door of No Return* from "A Circumstantial Account of a State of Things" to another kind of circumstantial account in her "Ruttier" for survival in the diaspora and in *Verso 55*. In Brand's work that door of no return marked the real and metaphorical site that "accounts for the ways we observe and are observed as people. It exists as the ground we walk. Every gesture our body makes somehow gestures toward this door" (Brand 2001, 26). In Brand's elaboration the door exists alongside and counter to the archive; it exists juxtapositionally as an account of the "thing in fact which we do not know about, a place we do not know. Yet it exists as the ground we walk." In the first instance, Brand (2001, 5) maps how we have come to live in the places we are and that "tear in the world" that is also "a rupture in history, a rupture in the quality of being." Brand maps a desire to say more than what is allowed by an archive that turns Black bodies into fungible flesh and deposits them there, betrayed. Brand began *Map* with that rupture, and she closes it with a song; the "Ruttier for the Marooned in the Diaspora" is her offering to guide us to how to live in the wake. The "Ruttier" is a guide to indiscipline and lawlessness; a map of disinheritance and inhabitation; a guide to how, traveling light, one might just live free of, "refuse, shut the door on," the weight of responsibility for one's planned demise. Simply, Brand's "Ruttier" insists us, Black people, into all of our largeness against that dysgraphia that would insist on the smallness of Black being in the wake. To do this, Brand plumbs the archives of the everyday that come from collecting, from thinking juxtapositionally, from "sitting in the room with history." *"They owe, own nothing. . . . They wander as if they have no century, as if they can bound time, as if they can sit in a café in Brugge just as soon as smoke grass in Tucson, Arizona, and chew coca in the high Andes for coldness"* (Brand 2001, 213–214).

Living with immi/a/nent death, in the shadow of that door, in the wake of slavery, with the obstructed passages of the Mediterranean, with carding, stop and frisk, the afterlives of partus sequitur ventrem, respiratory distress, detention centers, *Lagers*, prisons, and a multitude of other forms of surveillance, "I want to do more than recount the violence that deposited these traces in the archive" (Hartman 2008, 2). So, I turn again to the photo of the beautiful girl with the word *Ship* on her forehead and to two images by Roy DeCarava that seem to speak to and anticipate it.

The images come from the photo text *The Sound I Saw*. The first photograph is of a little Black boy, approximately five years old. The shot is close cropped, and it is his face that we see; it is his face that is in focus. His face occupies the majority of the frame. He looks to be wearing a hospital gown; the material seems to be gauze, it is white, and it has a V-neck. He is lying on a white or light-colored sheet. He has a small mark over his right eyebrow. He looks concerned; his brow is slightly furrowed. His look, like the look of the girl, reaches out to me across time and space. His big brown eyes look out at something, at someone, at and to us.

In *In the Wake: On Blackness and Being*, I wanted to make present the someone that those eyes look out to. I wanted to stay in the wake to sound an ordinary note of care. I name it an ordinary note because it takes as weather the contemporary conditions of Black life and death. Another one of the textual scenes that exemplify this note of care of which I speak, this ordinary sounding of care in excess of the places where we are, arrives through the character of Hi Man in Toni Morrison's *Beloved*. Hi Man is the "lead chain" of the gang of men in the prison chain gang to which Paul D is sold in Alfred, Georgia, after he is captured during his escape from Sweet Home:

> "Hiiii!" . . . It was the first sound, other than "Yes, sir" a blackman was allowed to speak each morning, and the lead chain gave it everything he had. "Hiiii!" It was never clear to Paul D how he knew when

to shout that Mercy. They called him Hi Man and Paul D thought at first the guards told him when to give that signal that let the prisoners rise up off their knees and dance two-step to the music of hand-forged iron. Later he doubted it. He believed to this day that the "Hiiii!" at dawn and the "Hoooo!" when evening came were the responsibility Hi Man assumed because he alone knew what was enough, what was too much, and when things were over, when the time had come. (Morrison 1987, 108)

Hi Man sounds and holds the note that keeps the men with whom he is chained from the brink. And when the deluge comes, the rain that almost kills them, locked underground in the mud and silt, in that cage called the slave ship on land—that note provides the means through which Paul D and the forty-five other men escape that prison ship in Alfred, Georgia.

The second DeCarava photograph is of a Black woman and that same little boy. She is facing away from the camera, and her face is turned toward the boy. She holds a thermometer in her right hand. In this photo the little boy is sitting up in the bed, cross-legged, in front of her. He is drinking water from a glass; she is watching him. His white top now seems to be a pajama top that matches the bottoms we now see that he has on. The photo's caption tells us that the woman is his mother. It doesn't look like they are in a hospital room. It looks like he is at home. There is a chest of drawers against the wall, and there are belongings on top of it. There is a grate in front of the window. I imagine the little girl with *Ship* taped to her forehead alongside this little boy from half a century before. The photographs are similar in subject; the little boy and the little girl bear a striking resemblance; she is a sick girl, he is a sick boy, they are both awaiting care. But Roy DeCarava took the photographs of the little boy and the little boy with the woman who is his mother: DeCarava, the famous Black photographer of Black life who refused the documentary, who refused to let his images of Black people be used to frame someone else's *not* seeing, to abet our thingification. So DeCarava's photographs are also strikingly different. And it is through the care and the light and shadow of DeCarava's look that this woman who is the little boy's mother appears, here, in a scene that strikes an ordinary note of care.

I return to Brand's "Ruttier for the Marooned in the Diaspora" as a song of direction that contains mercy, a song that contains all of the things that we are. Her "Ruttier" writes and contains Black being as it has developed in the wake; Black being that continually exceeds all of the violence directed at Black life; Black being that exceeds that force. For Brand, all of this is knowledge and wealth. And she offers us a song, a map to anywhere, to everywhere, in all of the places in which we find ourselves. The Ruttier: a map to be held; to behold.

So we are here in the weather, here in the singularity. Here there is disaster and possibility. And while *we are constituted through and by continued vulnerability to this overwhelming force, we are not only known to ourselves and to each other by that force.*"

NOTES

*

Chapter 1: The Wake

1 Some definitions, phrases, and quotations (like, for example, the definitions of wake) will repeat throughout the text of *In the Wake* and will be marked by italics. I imagine these italicized repetitions as a reminder, a refrain, and more.

2 I share this with a friend and he responds with the following: "I tripped over the word 'opportunity,' [in my narrative] because of its ubiquity in the narratives of Dutch Caribbeans. I've been thinking a lot about the work that 'opportunity' does both in Dutch Caribbean narratives of migration, and the Dutch government's pledge to 'create opportunities for all.' My parents moved to the Netherlands 'for opportunity,' and they also experienced 'constant and overt racism, isolation.' My father was kept in the same job with no prospect of promotion for years on end; ironically, in the Dutch Caribbean the Netherlands has been imagined as the 'land of opportunity' (and I won't be getting into how that imagination has been shaped by colonialism). The Netherlands has become fixed as an orientation point." Personal email cited with the permission of the author, Egbert Alejandro Martina.

3 A while ago when I was searching for something else in the archives of the *Philadelphia Inquirer* I found two of the many op-eds that my mother wrote and that were published in the paper after she read about, saw, or otherwise witnessed racism. I include the text of the letters here.

> Letters to the Editor: Deep-seated Bias
> December 20, 1986
>
> If anyone has seriously been entertaining doubts that deep-seated prejudice is alive and thriving in the United States, he has only to read the Dec. 9 front page article in The Inquirer concerning the 14-year-old girl who was a rape victim to disabuse himself of this naive notion.

Here we have a situation cast in the classic mold of the pre-civil rights era. A white female is raped (by a white male whom she knows) but, when describing her assailant, she does not describe a bogus white male but chooses to describe her attacker as a nonexistent black male. How sad that this 14-year-old child apparently instinctively chose a member (albeit a fictitious one) of another race to be her victim.

Ida Wright Sharpe
Wayne

Letters to the Editor: Racist Asides
March 02, 1992

While I sympathize with Jack Smith's son who was given a traffic ticket because of the flashing lights on his car (after all, are they any more distracting than the vanity plates that one tries to read in passing?), I am more concerned about the gratuitous comments made by Mr. Smith.

His remark that the car "looked as if it had just rolled out of the barrio" is blatantly racist, as is his question about the lights being "overly . . . Latino." Is one to believe, as Jack Smith apparently does, that on the Main Line only Spanish-speaking individuals drive cars that have anything other than the names of universities and yacht clubs embellishing the rear windows?

I don't know how long Jack Smith has been a resident of Wayne, but I have lived here for over 38 years and can assure him that 90 percent of the individuals whom I have seen over the years getting in and out of highly decorated vehicles have been white males of assorted ages.

In the meantime he needs to work on his racist assumptions about the other kids on the Main Line; some of them — many of them in fact — are not white and none of them deserves to be pigeon-holed and disparaged by people like Jack Smith.

Ida Wright Sharpe
Wayne

4 I draw the optic of the door from the work of Dionne Brand, who writes, in *A Map to the Door of No Return*, that the door of no return is on her retina. I return to this later in the introduction and throughout this text.
5 See the forthcoming book by Rinaldo Walcott, *The Long Emancipation*. Walcott names this unfinished project the long emancipation and he defines it thus: "It is the interdiction of a potential black freedom that I have termed the long emancipation."
6 For Blanchot the disaster is the Holocaust. For me it is the ongoing unfolding of centuries of the trade in Africans — an event that is historical and one that, as Dionne Brand writes, ruptures history. Morrison writes, "The overweening,

defining event of the modern world is the mass movement of raced popula-
tions, beginning with the largest forced transfer of people in the history of the
world: slavery. The consequences of which transfer have determined all the
wars following it as well as the current ones being waged on every continent."
See Morrison 1998; Blanchot 1995, 1–2.

7 Blanchot's translator notes that the writing of the disaster "means not simply
the process whereby something called the disaster is written — communicated,
attested to or prophesied. It also means the writing done by the disaster —
by the disaster that ruins books and wrecks language. "The writing of the disaster" means the writing that the disaster — which liquidates writing — is just
as 'knowledge of the disaster' means knowledge as disaster, and the 'flight of
thought' the loss of thought, which thinking is" (Ann Smock in Blanchot 1995,
ix).

8 I thank Mario DiPaolantonia for thinking this through with me after my talk at
York University.

9 In the premiere issue of *Lateral*, the online journal of the Cultural Studies Association, Jared Sexton writes the following on Lewis Gordon in *Ante-Anti-
Blackness: Afterthoughts*. "I am guided in the following task by a two-sided idea
derived from Gordon's arguments: 1) all thought, insofar as it is genuine thinking, might best be conceived of as black thought and, consequently, 2) all re-
searches, insofar as they are genuinely critical inquiries, aspire to black studies."
Sexton 2012.

10 Lexi Belcufine, "Turtle Creek 20-Year-Old Fatally Shot in Fineview," *Pittsburgh Post-Gazette*, December 10, 2013, http://www.post-gazette.com/local
/city/2013/12/10/Pittsburgh-police-responding-to-shooting-on-North-Side
/stories/201312100134.

11 Courier Newsroom, "65 of 91 Homicides Black Lives in 2013," *Pittsburgh Courier*,
January 8, 2014, http://newpittsburghcourieronline.com/2014/01/08/65-of-91
-homicides-black-lives-in-2013/.

12 My memory differs from my brother Christopher's here. Christopher recalls
that Robert was shot eleven times. Van Zimmerman and I each recall that
Robert was shot nineteen times.

13 My mother wrote a letter to the editor about Robert's murder and the way it
was reported in the news, but I have not been able to locate it. I include here
two letters that are in the *Philadelphia Inquirer*'s online archives and that point
to some of the ways my mother lived in the world.

14 "Big Steve — Lil Nigga Trey (lil nigga snupe beat)," YouTube video, 2:31,
December 17, 2013. https://www.youtube.com/watch?v=mv_dqwcOM5c&
feature=youtu.be.

15 "U.S. Marshals Arrest Pittsburgh Homicide Suspect in New Kensington,"
Pittsburgh Post-Gazette, March 28, 2014, http://www.post-gazette.com/local
/city/2014/03/28/U-S-Marshals-arrest-Pittsburgh-homicide-suspect-in-New
-Kensington/stories/201403280201.

I have redacted the name of the young Black man accused of murdering my nephew Caleb. It serves no purpose to name him here. I say more about what I am calling the practices of Black annotation and Black redaction in the final section of this work, "The Weather."

16 In Stein 2007 we read: "After lives in which they often struggle to get medical care, African Americans and other minorities are more likely than whites to want, and get, more aggressive care as death nears and are less likely to use hospice and palliative-care services to ease their suffering, according to a large body of research and leading experts.

As a result, they are more likely to experience more medicalized deaths, dying more frequently in the hospital, in pain, on ventilators and with feeding tubes — often after being resuscitated or getting extra rounds of chemotherapy, dialysis or other care, studies show."

See also Cardinale Smith and Otis Brawley, "Disparities in Access to Palliative Care," *Health Affairs Blog*, July 30, 2014, http://healthaffairs.org/blog/2014/07/30/disparities-in-access-to-palliative-care/. They write, "Even when socioeconomic status is the same, minority patients remain at risk for disparities in treatment for pain. Physicians appear to deliver less information and communicate less support to African-American and Hispanic patients compared to white patients, even in the same care settings. Furthermore, minority patients often do not receive treatment consistent with their wishes even when their wishes are known."

17 Silverstein (2013) writes: "The more privilege assumed of the target, the more pain the participants perceived. Conversely, the more hardship assumed, the less pain perceived."

18 That is, study within the university and graduate classroom and not Black Study as Moten and Harney take it up in *The Undercommons: Fugitive Planning and Black Study*.

19 Brand writes: "One enters a room and history follows; one enters a room and history precedes. History is already seated in the chair in the empty room when one arrives. Where one stands in a society seems always related to this historical experience. Where one can be observed is relative to that history. All human effort seems to emanate from this door. How do I know this? Only by self-observation, only by looking. Only by feeling. Only by being a part, sitting in the room with history" (Brand 2001, 29).

20 Wilderson (2010, 2) writes about "helping the manuscript to stay in the hold of the ship, despite my fantasies of flight."

21 I use "transmigration" here to mean movement across and also the movement from one form to another.

22 It appears, still, that within a particular ideological frame paternal responsibility remains a prerequisite to (right to) life.

23 "The Dominicans Use Drones to Hunt Down Undocumented Haitians," *Rezo Nodwes*, August 18, 2015, https://rezonodwes.com/les-dominicains-utilisent

-des-drones-pour-traquer-les-sans-papiers-haitiens/. The article reads, "The Dominican Minister of Defense, Lt. Gen. Máximo Williams Muñoz Delgado, announced the operationalization of 'a new border surveillance modality with [l'incorporation] drones to detect illegal migrants and traffickers all kinds. These new reconnaissance aircraft, equipped with advanced technology transmit a signal to two trucks prepared for the processing of images in real time and from which orders to depart (come) to hunt down illegal. The Dominicans use drones to hunt down undocumented Haitians. . . . Note that the Turks and Caicos Islands had also announced the use of these devices in their efforts to hunt Haitian boat people." (This is a rough translation of the original article through google translate).

24 See Sharpe 2012a, 828. As the sentence appears there it reads in part: "constituted through and by vulnerability to overwhelming force though not only known to themselves and to each other by that force."

25 *Verso 55* (Brand 2015) is unpublished; it is used here with permission of the author.

26 Hartman writes, "This writing is personal because this history has engendered me, because 'the knowledge of the other marks me,' because of the pain experienced in my encounter with the scraps of the archive, and because of the kinds of stories I have fashioned to bridge the past and the present and to dramatize the production of nothing—empty rooms, and silence, and lives reduced to waste" (Hartman 2008, 4).

27 R. M. Kennedy, in acknowledging the powers and the dangers of thinking melancholia, writes that melancholia, in its refusal of the outside, its refusal to bring into itself that outside object, forms a too-ready alignment with nationalist discourses. See Kennedy 2010.

28 From the euphemism of children forcibly removed from their parents into state "care" to laws like the "beyond the front door policy" in the Netherlands that forces people, often nonwhite, to open their doors to state monitoring and intrusion, to medical experiments and the forced feeding of hunger strikers, who for example, refuse food to protest *that* they are held *and* the conditions under which they are held. All of this and more is carried out under the rubric of care. Yet I want to find a way to hold onto something like care as a way to feel and to feel for and with, a way to tend to the living and the dying.

29 Lewis Gordon (2007, 11) makes clear that zone includes the disaster of recognition and "living with the possibility," not to say the necessity, "of one's arbitrary death as a legitimate feature of a system."

30 In an interview with Maya Mavjee about *A Map to the Door of No Return: Notes on Belonging*, poet, novelist, essayist Dionne Brand activates another understanding of luck. I offer it here. Brand says, "In *Map* I talk about all these interpretations that you walk into unknowingly, almost from birth. If you're lucky you spend the rest of your life fighting them, if you're not, you spend your life unquestioningly absorbing" (Brand and Mavjee 2001).

Chapter 2: The Ship

1 *The Forgotten Space*, http://www.theforgottenspace.net/static/home.html (accessed June 17, 2015).

2 I think here of those fish and those body parts of enslaved Africans in Turner's work but also Ellen Gallagher's *Blubber* (2000) and Kara Walker's *Middle Passages*, each of which make visceral the relation between Black people and any "fish (or water mammal) story." See also Rediker 2008.

3 Llenín-Figueroa (2014, 90) writes, "At first glance, the immediate present shows a Caribbean relationship with the sea mediated by the powerful machine of global capital: the tourism industry, both as a more or less established enterprise of hotels and resorts that has appropriated coastal regions and as a transient industry in the form of massive cruise ships that take over interinsular sea routes; the mobility of cheap labor migrating between Caribbean islands and toward the United States in *yolas* or *balsas*; the nodes of a global network of lucrative businesses, the most potent and deadly of which is, of course, drug trafficking; and the dumping site of capitalism's debris, waste, garbage, spills, and the excesses of its nuclear experiments and military operations."

4 Allan Sekula and Noël Burch, "The Forgotten Space," panel discussion, April 24, 2012, http://www.tate.org.uk/context-comment/video/allan-sekula-and -noel-burch-forgotten-space-panel-discussion.

5 Prior to her interview we have glimpsed her in the film as she appears in the background of several shots of the tent city. One must ask, and attempt to answer, why this one, of all of the film stills that one could use for the film. See Academy Lectures: Kunstakademiet Academy of Fine Art, http://academy lectures.khio.no/?page_id=53 (accessed July 5, 2015).

6 I return to this designation of "former mother" in the section of this book called "The Hold." I include three images of Aereile Jackson because I want to read these photo/text of her image and the films' use of it. Though she is in the film only for a very short period of time, I am interested in how her image circulates as one of the film's publicity stills. Of the images included here, one is a still from the film, and the other is from the end credits (and in this there is an echo of Steve McQueen's 2012 film on the FBI files of Paul Robeson called *End Credits*, to which I turn briefly in the section titled "The Weather"). The final image of Aereile Jackson appears in Darrell Varga 2012, "Making Political Cinema—The Forgotten Space."

7 Transcription mine.

8 S.v. "opportunity," *Dictionary Online*, http://www.dictionary.com/browse /opportune.

9 In "What More Can I Say? (A Prose-Poem on Antiblackness)," C. Riley Snorton (2014) writes, "To be not fully human—which seems to also mean to be something else (other/Other? super? sub?) and to survive—which means to be in excess (or perhaps outside) of life is a peculiarly black predicament."

10 Here I draw on Dionne Brand's formulation and theorization of the real and mythic Door of No Return as the site of Black Diaspora consciousness. She writes, "The door signifies the historical moment which colours all moments in the Diaspora. It accounts for the ways we observe and are observed as people, whether it's through the lens of social injustice or the lens of human accomplishments. The door exists as an absence. A thing in fact which we do not know about, a place we do not know. Yet it exists as the ground we walk. Every gesture our body makes somehow gestures toward this door. What interests me primarily is probing the Door of No Return as consciousness. The door casts a haunting spell on personal and collective consciousness in the Diaspora. Black experience in any modern city or town in the Americas is a haunting. One enters a room and history follows; one enters a room and history precedes. History is already seated in the chair in the empty room when one arrives. Where one stands in a society seems always related to this historical experience. Where one can be observed is relative to that history. All human effort seems to emanate from this door. How do I know this? Only by self-observation, only by looking. Only by feeling. Only by being a part, sitting in the room with history" (Brand 2001, 24–25).

I draw, too, on the work of Frank Wilderson, especially *Red, White, and Black* (2010), in which he argues that violence against the Black is gratuitous and not contingent; not violence that occurs between subjects at the level of conflict in the world but violence at the level of a structure that required, indeed invented, the Black to be the constitutive outside for those who would construct themselves as *the* Human.

11 Brooks (2010a) writes, "We're all supposed to politely respect each other's cultures. But some cultures are more progress-resistant than others, and a horrible tragedy was just exacerbated by one of them."

12 I turn more fully to the question of the singularity in the section called "The Weather."

13 And, as Marcus Rediker and others have told us, the captains and crew of any and every slave ship had to ready themselves for all forms of "creative resistance" by the captives (Rediker 2007, 307). And here is Walvin (2011, 107): "Every slave ship expected to face dangers from their African captives."

14 Sharpe (2010, 29) writes: "If 'slavery is the ghost in the machine of kinship,' it is in part because under slavery, system and sign, lexico-legal acts of transubstantiation occur in which blood becomes property (with all of the rights inherent in the use and enjoyment of property) in one direction and kin in another."

15 Philip writes, "Very early on I develop a need to know the names of the murdered and actually call James Walvin, author of *Black Ivory*, in England to ask him if he knew how I could locate them. 'Oh, no,' his tone is commiserative, 'they didn't keep names.' I don't—cannot believe this to be true, but later on as a result of correspondence with a colleague who is researching and writing a book on the *Zong* case, I receive a copy of a sales book kept by one Thomas

Case, an agent in Jamaica who did business with the owners of the *Zong*. It is typical of the records kept at that time: Purchasers are identified while Africans are reduced to the stark description of 'negroe man,' [*sic*] 'negroe woman,' or more frequently 'ditto man,' 'ditto woman.' There is one gloss to this description: 'Negroe girl (meagre).' There are many 'meagre' girls, no 'meagre' boys.

The African men, women, and children, on board the *Zong* were stripped of all specificity, including their names. Their financial value, however, was recorded and preserved for insurance purposes, each being valued at thirty pounds sterling" (Philip 2008, 194).

16   Interview with Dr. Anne Gardulski, July 7, 2014, Cambridge, MA.

17   I recognize that that title of first Black published poet goes to Jupiter Hammon. Wheatley is the first Black woman poet to publish in what will become the United States.

18   I expand, here, the argument I made in *Monstrous Intimacies*. "Agassiz was one of the founders (or fathers) of the American school of ethnology; he was an abolitionist and a contributor to the emergent field of racial science, who believed in African inferiority and European superiority. Pro-slavery politicians embraced his polygenetic arguments that attempted to make manifest, measurable, and readable an essential black inferiority and black monstrosity, not the monstrosity of slavery and slavery's complicated black performances and not the violence of the law and the gaze." And "the daguerreotypes (the 'mirror with a memory') commissioned by the abolitionist Agassiz that would be used to support slavery and to naturalize and justify the continued subjection of black people in and eventually out of slavery" (Sharpe 2010, 11–12).

19   There has been some dispute about the numbers of those thrown overboard. I indicate the discrepancy in numbers here.

20   "Despite the change in policy, the INS has continued to return Haitians leaving the country in small boats—over 1,300 boat people were returned to Haiti in May after the change in policy was announced." "Clinton Changes US Policy on Haitian Refugees," *Migration News* 1, 5 (June 1994), https://migration.ucdavis.edu/mn/more.php?id=328 (accessed July 7, 2015).

21   Again, the captions read: "An injured child waits to be flown for treatment on the USNS *Comfort*." And: "A child waits to be medevaced by U.S. Army soldiers from the 82nd Airborne to the USNS Comfort in Port-au-Prince, Haiti." "PORT-AU-PRINCE, HAITI—JANUARY 21: A child waits to be medevaced by U.S. Army soldiers from the 82nd Airborne to the USNS Comfort on January 21, 2010 in Port-au-Prince, Haiti. Planeloads of rescuers and relief supplies headed to Haiti as governments and aid agencies launched a massive relief operation after a powerful earthquake that may have killed thousands. Many buildings were reduced to rubble by the 7.0-strong quake on January 12."

22   The photographer, Joe Raedle, is from the United States.

23   Jack Shenker, "Migrants Left to Die after Catalogue of Failures, Says Report into Boat Tragedy," *Guardian*, March 28, 2012, http://www.theguardian.com

/world/2012/mar/28/left-to-die-migrants-boat-inquiry. I will return to this later in this section and in the sections "The Hold" and "The Weather."

24 See, for example, Schwartz 2010; Barron H. Lerner, "Scholars Argue over Legacy of Surgeon Who Was Lionized, Then Vilified," *New York Times*, October 28, 2003, http://www.nytimes.com/2003/10/28/health/scholars-argue -over-legacy-of-surgeon-who-was-lionized-then-vilified.html; Caitlin Dickerson, "Secret World War II Chemical Experiments Tested Troops by Race," *Morning Edition*, NPR, June 22, 2015, http://www.npr.org/2015/06/22/415194765 /u-s-troops-tested-by-race-in-secret-world-war-ii-chemical-experiments; Sophie Kleeman, "One Powerful Illustration Shows Exactly What's Wrong with How the West Talks about Ebola," *World.Mic*, October 7, 2014, http://mic .com/articles/100618/one-powerful-illustration-shows-exactly-what-s-wrong -with-media-coverage-of-ebola; Kathryn Krase, "History of Forced Sterilization and Current U.S. Abuses," Our Bodies Ourselves.org. October 1, 2014. http://www.ourbodiesourselves.org/health-info/forced-sterilization/.

25 Michael M. Phillips and Christopher Rhoads, "Government Turns to Long-Term Needs," *Wall Street Journal*, January 22, 2010, http://www.wsj.com /articles/SB10001424052748704423204575017384160415238.

26 Mary Beth Sheridan and Manuel Roig-Franzia, "Haiti Relief: 2,000 Tents—200,000 Needed," *SF Gate*, January 22, 2010, http://www.sfgate.com/world /article/Haiti-relief-2-000-tents-200-000-needed-3275233.php.

27 Definition: A Dictionary of Literary Devices (Gradus, A–Z).

28 Andrea Rose and Colleen Barry, "Italy Divers Find 'Wall' of Bodies in Migrant Ship," *Seattle Times*, October 8, 2013, http://www.seattletimes.com/nation -world/italy-divers-find-wall-of-bodies-in-migrant-ship/.

29 Gianluca Mezzofiore, "Lampedusa: Italian Fishermen 'Abandoned' Hundreds of African Migrants to Drown," *International Business Times*, October 3, 2013, http://www.ibtimes.co.uk/lampedusa-fishing-boats-turned-away-migrant -sinking-511190.

30 This is a reference to Dasani Coates who was featured in the *New York Times* special feature "Invisible Child." I discuss this in chapter 4, "The Weather."

31 For an in-depth analysis of the Black Mediterranean see Saucier and Woods 2014.

32 Ian Traynor, "EU to launch military operations against migrant-smugglers in Libya," *Guardian*, April 20, 2015, http://www.theguardian.com/world/2015/apr /20/eu-launch-military-operations-libya-migrant-smugglers-mediterranean.

33 "EU to Back 'Boat-Destroyer' Mission in Mediterranean," BBC *News*, May 18, 2015, http://www.bbc.com/news/world-europe-32776688. We read, "On May 18, 2015, the European Union voted to replace humanitarian patrols of the Mediterranean with military ones"

34 Corina Crețu, "Mémorial "ACTe: A Place of Remembrance and of Reconciliation," European Commission, February 8, 2015, https://ec.europa.eu /commission/2014–2019/cretu/blog/memorial-acte-place-remembrance -and-reconciliation_en.

35 "Hollande Honours the Lives of Slaves at Caribbean Museum," *France 24*, May 10, 2015, http://www.france24.com/en/20150510-france-slavery-hollande -caribbean-museum-guadeloupe.

36 In the prologue to *Invisible Man* the narrator says, "but that . . . is how the world moves: Not like an arrow, but a boomerang. (Beware of those who speak of the *spiral* of history; they are preparing a boomerang. Keep a steel helmet handy.)" (Ellison 1995, 6).

37 "Ark of Return: UN Erects Memorial to Victims of Transatlantic Slave Trade," UN News Centre, http://www.un.org/apps/news/story.asp?NewsID=50428.

38 Jocelyne Sambira, "Historic 'Ark of Return' Monument on Slavery Un- veiled at the UN," Africa Renewal Online. March 25, 2015. http://www.un.org /africarenewal/web-features/historic-%E2%80%98ark-return%E2%80%99 -monument-slavery-unveiled-un.

39 Charles Gaines, "Creative Time Summit: The Curriculum," Venice Biennale, August 11. 2015, http://livestream.com/creativetime/biennalearte/videos/95 991585.

Chapter 3: The Hold

1 Justice for Albert Johnson, Pushing Buttons, Pushing Stories, http://archives .library.yorku.ca/exhibits/show/pushingbuttons/social-activism/justice-for -albert-johnson (accessed July 15, 2015).

2 Jessica Elgot and Matthew Taylor, "Calais Crisis: Cameron Condemned for 'Dehumanising' Description of Migrants," *Guardian*, July 30, 2015, http://www .theguardian.com/uk-news/2015/jul/30/david-cameron-migrant-swarm -language-condemned.

See also Jessica Elgot and Patrick Wintour, "Calais: Man Killed as Migrants Make 1,500 Attempts to Enter Eurotunnel Site," *Guardian*, July 29, 2015, http:// www.theguardian.com/uk-news/2015/jul/29/calais-one-dead-1500-migrants -storm-eurotunnel-terminal.

Remember, too, that in 2008 Silvio Berlusconi referred to undocumented immigrants as an "army of evil." Malcolm Moore, "Silvio Berlusconi Says Illegal Migrants Are 'Army of Evil,'" *Telegraph*, April 16, 2008, http://www.telegraph .co.uk/news/worldnews/1895799/Silvio-Berlusconi-says-illegal-migrants-are -army-of-evil.html.

3 "Quotes from, and about, Nicolas Sarkozy," *New York Times*, May 7, 2007, http://www.nytimes.com/2007/05/07/world/europe/07francequotes.html The Kärcher has particular resonance with Algerian uprisings in France.

4 Justin Huggler, "Buchenwald Concentration Camp Immigration Plan Criti- cised," *Telegraph*, January 13, 2015, http://www.telegraph.co.uk/news/world news/europe/germany/11343119/Buchenwald-concentration-camp-immi gration-plan-criticised.html. "Plans to house asylum seekers in a former SS bar- racks at a Nazi concentration camp are causing controversy in Germany."

5 Yermi Brenner, "Asylum Seekers Face Increasing Violence in Germany," *Al Jazeera*, June 6, 2015, http://america.aljazeera.com/articles/2015/6/15/asylum-seekers-face-increasing-violence-in-germany.html.

6 Daniel Trilling, "In Germany, Refugees Seek Fair Treatment," *Al Jazeera*, April 3, 2014, http://www.aljazeera.com/indepth/features/2014/04/germany-refugees-seek-fair-treatment-berlin-oranienplatz-20144211253138114.html.

7 "Greek Police Spray Migrants with Fire Extinguishers," *Al Jazeera*, August 11, 2015, http://www.aljazeera.com/news/2015/08/greek-police-kos-migrants-150811124542301.html.

8 Oumar Bar, "When Senegalese Writer Fatou Diome Kicked European Union Butt," *Africa Is a Country*, April 2015, http://africasacountry.com/2015/04/that-moment-when-senegalese-writer-fatou-diome-kicked-european-union-butt/.

9 In Wright's encounter with the disfiguring coffle (or chain-gang) of black male prisoners who he, at first recognizes not as men but as a row of elephants chained together, these men are transformed into something else — not men but elephant. The only men he recognizes as men are the white men guarding the black men on the gang (Wright 2007, 57–58).

10 "In November 1994, . . . the North Carolina Department of Correction (DOC) issued a press release announcing that it had unearthed a relic of America's carceral past at one of its facilities. The release read in part: "[The] Community Resource Council for the Alexander Correctional Center arranged for the National Guard to forklift the cage out of the mud and vines. The original three-inch concrete floor, a small toilet and braided metal bars are all that remain of the prison cage where twelve convicts slept." Dennis Childs. 2015. *Slaves of the State*.

11 S.v. "ana-," OED *Online*.

12 "12 Yr. Old Girl Beaten by Police; Mistaken for a Prostitute," *Daily Kos*, February 11, 2009, http://www.dailykos.com/story/2009/02/11/696018/-UPDATE-4-12-yr-old-girl-beaten-by-police-mistaken-for-a-prostitute.

13 Darren Wilson, 2014. Grand Jury testimony, *Washington Post*, November 26, https://www.washingtonpost.com/apps/g/page/national/read-darren-wilsons-full-grand-jury-testimony/1472/.

14 Remember, for example, Tanya McDowell, who was arrested and convicted of "stealing education" for her children by registering them for school using an address that was not her own. See Daniel Tepfer, "Tanya McDowell Sentenced to 5 Years in Prison," March 27, 2012, *Connecticut Post*, http://www.ctpost.com/news/article/Tanya-McDowell-sentenced-to-5-years-in-prison-3437974.php.

15 See Kamau Brathwaite's "Dream Haiti." The formal innovations and the different versions of Brathwaite's work always present difficulty for reproduction.

16 Taylor Lewis, "Black Mother Found Dead in Jail Cell after Alerting Officials of Her Health Problems," *Essence*, July 29, 2015, http://www.essence.com/2015/07/29/black-mother-found-dead-jail-cell-after-alerting-officials-health-problems.

17 Tim Hume, "Young Brothers, 'Denied Refuge,' Swept to Death by Sandy," CNN, November 4, 2012, http://www.cnn.com/2012/11/02/world/americas/sandy -staten-island-brothers/.

18 Jake Tapper, "William Bennett Defends Comment on Abortion and Crime," ABC News, September 29, 2005, http://abcnews.go.com/WNT/Politics/story ?id=1171385.

19 The American Psychological Association released a report in 2014 that concluded, "Black boys as young as 10 may not be viewed in the same light of childhood innocence as their white peers, but are instead more likely to be mistaken as older, be perceived as guilty and face police violence if accused of a crime.... Children in most societies are considered to be in a distinct group with characteristics such as innocence and the need for protection. Our research found that black boys can be seen as responsible for their actions at an age when white boys still benefit from the assumption that children are essentially innocent.... Researchers used questionnaires to assess the participants' prejudice and dehumanization of blacks. They found that participants who implicitly associated blacks with apes thought the black children were older and less innocent" (Goff 2014).

20 "Two teenage sweethearts suspected in a crime spree of stolen vehicles and pilfered checks across the South have been taken into custody in Florida, Kentucky authorities said Sunday. Grayson County sheriff's officials say in a statement that 18-year-old Dalton Hayes and his 13-year-old girlfriend, Cheyenne Phillips, were arrested without incident about 12:10 a.m. local time Sunday in Panama City Beach. The two had eluded police in multiple states while raising concern about their increasingly bold behavior. Some media outlets had described the pair as a modern-day Bonnie and Clyde, the Depression-era lovebird outlaws." Associated Press, "Police Capture Teen 'Bonnie and Clyde' Suspected in a Trail of Crime," LA Times, January 18, 2015, http://www.latimes .com/nation/nationnow/la-na-teen-sweethearts-kentucky-20150118-story .html.

21 Where Black people are concerned, at least in the United States, the only instances of crime being rearranged into romance that come to mind are when the criminal is white, the assailed is Black, and the crime is slavery and rape in slavery, whereby the question of crime is to be suspended by a grammar of love. I offer Thomas Jefferson and Sally Hemings as the prime example. This is so much the case that in an episode of the cable show Homeland the daughter, Dana, signs herself Sally in messages to the vice president's son, whom she calls Thomas.

22 Charlie LeDuff, "What Killed Aiyana Stanley-Jones?" Mother Jones, November/December 2010, http://www.motherjones.com/politics/2010/11/aiyana -stanley-jones-detroit.

23 "The prosecution noted that even having his finger on the trigger of his submachine gun was improper." "Charges Dropped for Cop Who Fatally Shot

Sleeping 7-Year-Old Girl," *Counter Current News*, November 30, 2014, http://countercurrentnews.com/2014/11/aiyana-stanley-jones/.

24 Rose Hackman, "She Was Only a Baby': Last Charge Dropped in Police Raid That Killed Sleeping Detroit Child," *Guardian*, January 31, 2015, http://www.theguardian.com/us-news/2015/jan/31/detroit-aiyana-stanley-jones-police-officer-cleared.

25 Darren Wilson, Grand Jury testimony, *Washington Post*, November 26, http://apps.washingtonpost.com/g/page/national/read-darren-wilsons-full-grand-jury-testimony/1472/.

26 See this PDF from the New York Civil Liberties Union (NYCLU): New York Civil Liberties Union, http://www.nyclu.org/files/Stop-and-Frisk_0.pdf (accessed March 2015).

27 Jennifer Smith Richards and Lori Kurtzman, "Are Police Going Too Far or Doing Their Job?," *Columbus Dispatch*, August 2, 2015, http://www.dispatch.com/content/stories/local/2015/08/02/going-too-far-or-doing-their-job.html.

28 Julie Dressner and Edwin Martinez, "The Scars of Stop and Frisk," *New York Times*, June 12, 2012, http://www.nytimes.com/2012/06/12/opinion/the-scars-of-stop-and-frisk.html?_r=3.

29 Kate Taylor, "Stop-and-Frisk Policy 'Saves Lives,' Mayor Tells Black Congregation," *New York Times*, June 10, 2012, http://www.nytimes.com/2012/06/11/nyregion/at-black-church-in-brooklyn-bloomberg-defends-stop-and-frisk-policy.html.

30 Dani McLain, "Black Women Vilified as a 'Lesbian Wolf Pack' Speak for Themselves in a New Film," *The Nation*, July 2, 2015, http://www.thenation.com/article/black-women-vilified-as-a-lesbian-wolf-pack-speak-for-themselves-in-new-film/. The *Nation* article reports that the "*New York Times* ran a headline that implied that a benign encounter had gone wrong because some woman couldn't lighten up: 'Man is stabbed in attack after admiring a stranger.'"

31 Colleen Long, "NYPD Operation Clean Halls Challenged in Court; Program Allows Police Inside Private Buildings," *Huffington Post*, March 11, 2013, http://www.huffingtonpost.com/2013/03/11/nypd-operation-clean-halls_n_2852097.html.

32 Logan Burruss, "New York Police Sued over Residential Building Patrols," CNN, March 29, 2012, http://www.cnn.com/2012/03/29/justice/new-york-police-lawsuit/. See also the report from the NYCLU on the class action lawsuit: "Class Action Lawsuit Challenges NYPD Patrols of Private Apartment Buildings," March 28, 2012, http://www.nyclu.org/news/class-action-lawsuit-challenges-nypd-patrols-of-private-apartment-buildings.

33 Wendy Ruderman, "Rude or Polite, City's Officers Leave Raw Feelings in Stops," *New York Times*, June 26, 2012, http://www.nytimes.com/2012/06/27/nyregion/new-york-police-leave-raw-feelings-in-stops.html.

34 Helen A. S. Popkin, "On Facebook, Teacher Calls Kids 'Future Criminals,'"

Today, April 5, 2011, http://www.today.com/money/facebook-teacher-calls
-kids-future-criminals-123949.

35 John Hurdle, "A Hospital Offers a Grisly Lesson on Gun Violence," *New York
    Times,* July 2, 2013, http://www.nytimes.com/2013/02/07/us/07philly.html?_r.
    "'Our goal here isn't to scare you straight,' Mr. Charles told them. 'We're just
    trying to give you an education.'" Despite Mr. Charles's assurances, it seems
    that the program, like much of US education directed at black and blackened
    peoples, is precisely in the model of *Scared Straight's* education in/as terror.

36 Cradle2Grave Program. 2013. Temple University Health System, Inc. http://
    www.cradletograveprogram.com/.

37 Cradle2Grave Program. 2013. Temple University Health System, Inc. http://
    www.cradletograveprogram.com/content/c2g_video1.htm.

38 Center for Nonviolence and Social Justice, 2014. http://www.nonviolenceand
    socialjustice.org/Healing-Hurt-People/29/. "Healing Hurt People (HHP) is
    the cornerstone program of the Center for Nonviolence and Social Justice.
    HHP is a community-focused, hospital-based program designed to reduce re-
    injury and retaliation among youth ages eight to thirty. The program is affili-
    ated with the Emergency Department (ED) at Hahnemann University Hospi-
    tal and the Drexel University College of Medicine. In the fall of 2009, HHP was
    expanded to St. Christopher's Hospital for Children to reach young victims of
    violence age eight to twenty-one.

    HHP works with clients who are seen in the ED for intentional injuries (gun-
    shot, stab, or assault wounds). The program was conceived by an interdisci-
    plinary team consisting of an emergency physician, an internist, a psychiatrist,
    a social worker, and a psychologist with extensive expertise in violence pre-
    vention and trauma. HHP was designed to address the needs—physical, emo-
    tional, and social—that victims of violence face after being released from the
    emergency department."

39 While the *Times* profile did not reveal Dasani's surname, she was later identi-
    fied as Dasani Coates when she appeared as a guest at the swearing in of Leticia
    James as New York City's Public Advocate.

40 Since the publication of the feature on Dasani, her family, and many of the
    other families who lived in Auburn have been moved and rehoused elsewhere.
    Andrea Elliott and Rebecca R. Ruiz, "New York Is Removing over 400 Chil-
    dren from 2 Homeless Shelters," *New York Times,* February 21, 2014, http://
    www.nytimes.com/2014/02/21/nyregion/new-york-is-removing-over-400
    -children-from-2-homeless-shelters.html.

41 Simone Browne writes, "If we are to take transatlantic slavery as the antecedent
    of contemporary surveillance technologies and practices as they concern in-
    ventories of ships' cargo and the making of 'scaled inequalities' in the Brookes
    slave ship schematic, biometric identification by branding the body with hot
    irons, slave markets and auction blocks as exercises of synoptic power where
    the many watched the few, slave passes and patrols, black codes and fugitive

slave notices, it is to the archives, slave narratives and often to black expressive practices and creative texts that we can look to for moments of refusal and critique. What I am arguing here is that with certain acts of cultural production we can find performances of freedom and suggestions of alternatives to ways of living under a routinized surveillance that was terrifying in its effects" (Browne 2012, 547).

42 See Katherine Schulten and Amanda Christy Brown, "The Learning Network: Teaching and Learning with the *New York Times*, Reading Club, 'Invisible Child,'" *New York Times*, December 12, 2013, http://learning.blogs.nytimes .com/2013/12/12/reading-club-invisible-child/: "Once a semester, we choose an important, long-form *New York Times* article that we think young people should read, and we invite anyone age 13 to 19 to come to the Learning Network blog and discuss it. We have a few ground rules for this feature, which we call Reading Club, but our main goal is to inspire thoughtful conversation."

43 See Colin Campbell and Ross Barkan, "Bloomberg Defends Homeless Policies while Calling Dasani Story 'Extremely Atypical,'" *Observer News*, December 17, 2013, http://politicker.com/2013/12/bloomberg-defends-citys-homeless -policies-calling-dasani-story-extremely-atypical/.

44 William, "I, Too, Am One of the Estimated 22,000 Homeless Children in New York," *Guardian*, "Comment Is Free" section, January 1, 2014, http://www .theguardian.com/commentisfree/2014/jan/01/homeless-student-new-york -city-speaks.

45 I return here to Maya Mavjee's interview with Dionne Brand and her understanding of luck. I repeat, "If you're lucky you spend the rest of your life fighting them, if you're not, you spend your life unquestioningly absorbing" (Brand 2001).

46 Change.Org. 2012. Aisha Truss-Miller & Family with the Black Youth Project, https://www.change.org/p/president-obama-make-a-speech-in-chicago -addressing-the-crisis-of-gun-violence.

47 This quotation is attributed to Professor Cathy Cohen. David Boroff, "Petition Urges President Obama to Visit Chicago in Wake of Hadiya Pendleton Murder," *New York Daily News*, February 7, 2013, http://www.nydailynews.com /news/politics/petition-urges-president-obama-visit-chicago-article-1.1257756.

48 President Barack Obama, ABC News, 18:07, December 16, 2012, http://abcnews .go.com/US/video/president-obama-speaks-newtown-conn-shooting-vigil -full-17994987.

49 See Sharpe 2015. I reprise here part of what I wrote in that article. Simultaneous with the televised event of the State of the Union (SOTU) was the televised murder of former LAPD officer Christopher Dorner. Dorner is alleged to have killed three people and before the full force of the state of California is mobilized to hunt him and eventually burn him to death, Christopher Dorner, too, believed in that phrase that Obama uses so often, "a more perfect union." As I watched the SOTU I fully expected the manhunt for Christopher Dorner

to appear, like OJ's white Bronco, as an inset at the bottom of the screen. Or for the spectacle of the "fight" to capture Dorner—though two hundred LAPD officers, ten other agencies, a Sno-Cat, helicopters, armored vehicles, and heat-seeking technology against one man can hardly be considered a fight; that (to quote Baby Suggs in *Beloved*) is a rout—to altogether replace the spectacle of the Black president's speech. Such is the compulsive orthography of the wake which has to reinvigorate, and palimpsestically inscribe, the fugitive enslaved over the im/possibility of the black president talking.

For more on Christopher Dorner, see Davey D Hip hop and Politics, February 7, 2013, http://hiphopandpolitics.wordpress.com/2013/02/07/uncensored -manifesto-from-retired-lapd-officer-christopher-dorner. See also Keguro Macharia, Gukira With(out) Predicates, February 15, 2013, https://gukira.word press.com/2013/02/15/christopher-dorners-love-letter/.

50 President Barack Obama, State of the Union Address (transcript), White House, February 12, 2013, https://www.whitehouse.gov/the-press-office/2013/02/12 /remarks-president-state-union-address.

51 Jeffries, "Obama's Chicago Speech Can't Address Gun Violence Unless It Takes on Race."

52 Obama talks in Chicago about Violence, Economy, February 15, 2013, Chicago at Hyde Park Academy, YouTube Video, 30:08, https://www.youtube.com/watch ?v=Mj_I12hfLhU.

53 Text of President Obama's Chicago Speech, February 15, 2013, NBC Chicago, http://www.nbcchicago.com/blogs/ward-room/president-obama-speech -chicago-191471731.html#ixzz2M9YxVYT6.

54 This is a reprisal of Charlotte Delbo's (1995) demand "Try to look. Try to see." Here I mean it to call up that which challenges the knowledges that one has come to accept—structured, for the Black, on the refusal of the ontological site of blackness.

Chapter 4: The Weather

1 The *Alligator* and *Voador* and *Voadora* were laden 100 percent with children. The Trans-Atlantic Slave Trade Database. http://www.slavevoyages.org/.

2 The Trans-Atlantic Slave Trade Database. http://www.slavevoyages.org/.

3 Steven Weisenburger, "A Historical Margaret Garner," http://margaretgarner. org/AHistoricalMargaretGarner.pdf: "When she was seven the Gaines family took Margaret along for a two-day shopping spree in Cincinnati, a sojourn on free-soil that would become a key point of legal contention at her 1856 fugitive slave trial."

4 Lizzie Dearden, "The Darker Your Skin—The Further Down You Go: The Hierarchical System aboard Italy's Migrant Boats That Governs Who Lives and Who Dies," *Independent*, April 22, 2015, http://www.independent.co.uk /news/world/europe/the-paler-your-skin—the-higher-up-you-go-the

-hierarchical-system-aboard-italys-migrant-boats-that-governs-who-lives-and
-who-dies-10193130.html.

5 "Los Angeles Police Reconsider Using Choke Hold," *New York Times*, September 2, 1991, http://www.nytimes.com/1991/09/03/us/los-angeles-police
-reconsider-using-choke-hold.html.

6 "Los Angeles Police Reconsider Using Choke Hold," *New York Times*, September 3, 1991, http://www.nytimes.com/1991/09/03/us/los-angeles-police
-reconsider-using-choke-hold.html.

7 Caroline Bankoff, "The Chokehold Situation in NYC Is Not Good," *New York
Magazine*, September 28, 2014, http://nymag.com/daily/intelligencer/2014
/09/chokehold-situation-in-nyc-is-not-good.html. See also "A Mutated Rule:
Lack of Enforcement in the Face of Persistent Chokehold Complaints in New
York City (An Evaluation of Chokehold Allegations Against Members of the
NYPD from January 2009 through June 2014)," New York City Civilian Com-
plaint Review Board. October 7, 2014, http://www.nyc.gov/html/ccrb/down
loads/pdf/Chokehold%20Study_20141007.pdf.

8 Susanna Capelouto, "Eric Garner: The Haunting Last Words of a Dying Man,"
CNN, December 4, 2014, http://www.cnn.com/2014/12/04/us/garner-last
-words/.

9 Mary M. Chapman, "Theodore Wafer Sentenced to 17 Years in Michigan
Shooting of Renisha McBride," *New York Times*, September 4, 2015, http://
www.nytimes.com/2014/09/04/us/theodore-wafer-sentenced-in-killing-of
-renisha-mcbride.html.

10 Lizette Alvarez and Cara Buckley, "Zimmerman Is Acquitted in Trayvon Martin
Killing," *New York Times*, July 13, 2013, http://www.nytimes.com/2013/07/14
/us/george-zimmerman-verdict-trayvon-martin.html.

11 "50 Migrants Die of Suffocation in the Hold," *TVM*, August 26, 2015, http://
www.tvm.com.mt/en/news/50-migrants-die-of-suffocation-in-hold/.

12 S.v. "imaging," *OED Online*.

13 I am suspending, here, a conversation about the ethics of the photographer.
Kimberly Juanita Brown tackles this subject exceptionally well in her powerful
and difficult essay "Regarding the Pain of the Other" (2014).

14 I have modified this framing and phrasing from Charlotte Delbo's outraged response and charge, in *Auschwitz and After* (1995), to Christians and others who
presume to "know."

15 Here, of course, I refer to the enslaved women captured by Zealy's camera for
Agassiz. Delia and Drana are the "country born" (meaning born in the United
States and not in Guinea or Congo) daughters of Renty and Jack, two of the
enslaved men who are also caught by and in Zealy's photographic process. I say
more about this in the section called "The Ship."

16 The seven daguerreotypes that were recovered in a drawer of the Peabody Museum at Harvard in the 1970s include images of the men sitting and standing,
half naked and fully naked, front, side, rear. The images of the two women, the

daughters, Delia and Drana, are of them front, dress pulled down and tucked in, and standing side. No images of them naked front, side, rear have been recovered. There are, however, images of an enslaved woman from Brazil that Agassiz commissioned and she is shot, captured, held, completely naked, front, back, side. There is no reason to think that such images of Delia and Drana do not exist. There is nothing that would have protected them.

17 I try to find out more. I try to contact the photographer. Finally, I get in touch, again, with Getty Images. Through them I ask the photographer if he knows what happened to this little girl. I ask if there were other people there waiting for evacuation with the word *Ship* affixed to their foreheads. Getty Images contacts Joe Raedle and they relay my questions to him. This is the answer I receive: "The photo was taken near the ruins of the presidential palace. The U.S. military was using the area as a staging site to transfer injured people out to the USNS Comfort on January 21, 2010 in Port-au-Prince, Haiti. Many other people were also being transported to the ship but I wouldn't know how many. I don't know where she is today, it's a long shot, but maybe if Christina contacts the PAO from the 82nd Airborne he may be able to help."

18 Tanzina Vega, "Schools' Discipline for Girls Differs by Race and Hue," *New York Times*, November 12, 2014, http://www.nytimes.com/2014/12/11/us /school-discipline-to-girls-differs-between-and-within-races.html.

19 James Roberts, *The Narrative of James Roberts a Soldier under Gen. Washington in the Revolutionary War* (1858), *Documenting the American South*, posted 2001, http://docsouth.unc.edu/neh/roberts/roberts.html.

20 John Hiscock, "Steve McQueen: 'This Film, for Me, Is about Love,'" *Telegraph*, March 3, 2014, http://www.telegraph.co.uk/culture/film/10525932/Steve -McQueen-This-film-for-me-is-about-love.html.

21 "Sissako says, "Zabou, the character she plays really exists: she lives in Gao and is a former dancer from *Crazy Horse* back in the 60s. She went crazy and started to dress like in the movie. She always has a cockerel on her shoulder and she speaks very good French. When the jihadists were in Gao, she was the only one who could walk around with her head uncovered, the only one who could sing, dance, smoke, and tell them they were 'assholes.' In other words, all that is forbidden is allowed when someone goes crazy. She is the embodiment of women who have borne the struggle; of those who have dared to resist." Watershed, Conversations about Cinema: Impact of Conflict, May 28, 2015, http://www .conversationsaboutcinema.co.uk/ioc/timbuktu/671/a-film-is-a-conversation -interview-with-abderrahmane-sissako/.

22 I am here referring, again, to Maurice Blanchot.

23 Oumar Bar, "When Senegalese Writer Fatou Diome Kicked European Union Butt," *Africa Is a Country*, April 2015, http://africasacountry.com/2015/04/that -moment-when-senegalese-writer-fatou-diome-kicked-european-union-butt/.

24 Biennale newspaper. The paper has no name. It was distributed in the German Pavilion at the 2015 Venice Biennale.

REFERENCES

*

Alexander, Elizabeth. 1995. "'Can You Be Black and Look at This?': Reading the Rodney King Video." In *Black Male: Representations of Masculinity in Contemporary Art*, edited by Thelma Golden, 90–110. New York: Whitney Museum of Art.

Armstrong, Tim. 2010. "Slavery, Insurance, and Sacrifice in the Black Atlantic." In *Sea Changes: Historicizing the Ocean*, edited by K. Bernhard, 167–185. New York: Routledge.

Azoulay, Ariella. 2008. *The Civil Contract of Photography*. Zone Books. Cambridge, MA: MIT Press.

Baucom, Ian. 2005. *Specters of the Atlantic: Finance Capital, Slavery, and the Philosophy of History*. Durham, NC: Duke University Press.

Bell, Beverly. 2013. *Fault Lines: Views across Haiti's Divide*. Foreword by Edwidge Danticat. Ithaca, NY: Cornell University Press.

Blanchot, Maurice. 1995. *The Writing of the Disaster*. Translated by Ann Smock. Lincoln: University of Nebraska Press.

Bolster, W. Jeffrey. 1998. *Black Jacks: African American Seamen in the Age of Sail*. Cambridge, MA: Harvard University Press.

Brand, Dionne. 2015. *Verso 55*. Unpublished. Quoted with permission of the author.

———. 2014. *Love Enough*. Toronto: Knopf Canada.

———. 2010. *Ossuaries*. Toronto: McClelland and Stewart.

———. 2006. *Inventory*. Toronto: McClelland and Stewart.

———. 2002. *Thirsty*. Toronto: McClelland and Stewart.

———. 2001. *A Map to the Door of No Return: Notes to Belonging*. Toronto: Doubleday Canada.

Brathwaite, Edward, and Nathaniel Mackey. 1999. *Conversations with Nathaniel Mackey: An Evening with Nate Mackey & Kamau Brathwaite 18 Nov. 1993*. We Press.

Brathwaite, Kamau. 2007. *DS (2): Dreamstories*. New York: New Directions.

————. 1994. *Middle Passages*. New York: New Directions.

Brand, Dionne, with Mavjee, Maya. 2001. "Opening the Door: An Interview with Dionne Brand." Randomhouse.com, http://www.randomhouse.com/high school/catalog/display.pperl?isbn=9780385258920&view=printqa.

Braun, Lundy. 2014. *Breathing Race into the Machine: The Surprising Career of the Spirometer from Plantation to Genetics*. Minneapolis: University of Minnesota Press.

Braun, Lundy, and Hamza Shaban. 2014. "How Racism Creeps into Medicine." *The Atlantic*, August 29, http://www.theatlantic.com/health/archive/2014 /08/how-racism-creeps-into-medicine/378618/.

Brooks, David. 2010a. "The Underlying Tragedy." January 15, http://www.nytimes .com/2010/01/15/opinion/15brooks.html?_r=0.

————. 2010b. "The Tel Aviv Cluster." January 12, http://www.nytimes.com/2010 /01/12/opinion/12brooks.html.

Brown, Kimberly Juanita. 2014. "Regarding the Pain of the Other: Photography, Famine, and the Transference of Affect." In *Feeling Photography*, edited by Elspeth H. Brown and Thy Phu, 181–203. Durham, NC: Duke University Press.

Brown, Vincent. 2008. *The Reaper's Garden: Death and Power in the World of Atlantic Slavery*. Cambridge, MA: Harvard University Press.

Browne, Simone. 2012. "Everybody's Got a Little Light under the Sun: Black Luminosity and the Visual Culture of Surveillance." *Cultural Studies* 26, no. 4: 542–564.

Burch, Noël, and Allan Sekula. 2011. "The Forgotten Space." *New Left Review* 69 (May–June), http://newleftreview.org/II/69/allan-sekula-noel-burch-the -forgotten-space.

————, dir. 2010. *The Forgotten Space—A Film Essay Seeking to Understand the Contemporary Maritime World in Relation to the Symbolic Legacy of the Sea*. Doc.Eye Film.

Campt, Tina M. 2012. *Image Matters: Archive, Photography, and the African Diaspora in Europe*. Durham, NC: Duke University Press.

Carter, J. Kameron. 2013. "Paratheological Blackness." *South Atlantic Quarterly* 112, no. 4: 589–611.

Chance, Matthew. 2013. "Lampedusa Boat Sinking: Survivors Recall Awful Ordeal." October 9, http://www.cnn.com/2013/10/08/world/europe/italy -lampedusa-boat-sinking/.

Childs, Dennis. 2015. *Slaves of the State: Black Incarceration from the Chain Gang to the Penitentiary*. Minneapolis: University of Minnesota Press.

————. 2009. "You Ain't Seen Nothin' Yet": *Beloved*, the American Chain Gang, and the Middle Passage Remix." *American Quarterly* 61, no. 2: 271–298.

Coates, Ta-Nehisi. 2015. *Between the World and Me*. New York: Spiegel & Grau.

Cooper, Helene. 2015. "Grim History Traced in Sunken Slave Ship Found off South Africa." May 31, http://www.nytimes.com/2015/06/01/world/africa /tortuous-history-traced-in-sunken-slave-ship-found-off-south-africa.html.

Copeland, Huey. 2013. *Bound to Appear: Art, Slavery, and the Site of Blackness in Multicultural America*. Chicago: University of Chicago Press.

Danticat, Edwidge. 2014. *Claire of the Sea Light*. New York: Vintage.

———. 1996a. *Krik? Krak!* New York: Vintage.

———. 1996b. "We Are Ugly, But We Are Here." *Caribbean Writer* 10: n.p., http://www.thecaribbeanwriter.org/view-volumes/?id=586.

Dash, Julie. 1992. *Daughters of the Dust: The Making of an African American Woman's Film*. New York: New Press.

———. 1991. *Daughters of the Dust*. New York: Kino.

D'Augiar, Fred. 2015. *Children of Paradise: A Novel (P.S.)*. New York: Harper Perennial.

———. 2000. *Feeding the Ghosts*. New York: Ecco.

Davies, Lizzie. 2013. "Lampedusa Victims Include Mother and Baby Attached by Umbilical Cord." *The Guardian*, October 10, http://www.theguardian.com/world/2013/oct/10/lampedusa-victims-mother-baby-umbilical-cord?CMP=twt_fd.

Dayan, Joan. 1999. "Held in the Body of the State: Prisons and the Law." In *History, Memory, and the Law*, edited by Austin Sarat and Thomas Kearns, 183–248. Ann Arbor: University of Michigan Press.

Dearden, Lizzie. 2015a. "The Darker Your Skin — The Further Down You Go: The Hierarchical System Aboard Italy's Migrant Boats That Governs Who Lives and Who Dies." April 21, http://www.independent.co.uk/news/world/europe/the-paler-your-skin-the-higher-up-you-go-the-hierarchical-system-aboard-italys-migrant-boats-that-10193130.html.

———. 2015b. "Migrant Boat Disaster: Captain Charged with Killing Passengers by Ramming Vessel into Ship." April 21, http://www.independent.co.uk/news/world/europe/migrant-boat-disaster-captain-charged-with-killing-passengers-by-ramming-vessel-into-ship-10192649.html.

Delbo, Charlotte. 1995. *Auschwitz and After*. New Haven, CT: Yale University Press.

DeLoughrey, Elizabeth M. 2010. "Heavy Waters: Waste and Atlantic Modernity." *PMLA* 125, no. 3: 703–712.

———. 2007. *Routes and Roots: Navigating Caribbean and Pacific Island Literatures*. Honolulu: University of Hawaii Press.

Diawara, Manthia. 2011. "One World in Relation: Édouard Glissant in Conversation with Manthia Diawara." *Nka, Journal of Contemporary African Art* 2011, no. 28: 4–19.

Douglass, Frederick. 1855/2003a. *My Bondage and My Freedom*. New York: Penguin Classics.

———. 1845/2003b. *Narrative of the Life of Frederick Douglass, an American Slave, Written by Himself*. Boston: Bedford / St. Martin's.

Douglass, Patrice and Frank Wilderson. 2013. "The Violence of Presence: Metaphysics in a Blackened World." *The Black Scholar* 43, no. 4.

Dupriez, B. M. 1991. *A Dictionary of Literary Devices: Gradus, AZ*. University of Toronto Press.

Eady, Cornelius. 2001. *Brutal Imagination*. New York: G. P. Putnam's Sons.

Elliott, Andrea. 2013. "Invisible Child: Dasani's Homeless Life in the Shadows." *New York Times*, December 9, http://www.nytimes.com/projects/2013/invisible-child/.

Ellison, Ralph. 1995. *Invisible Man*. New York: Vintage.

English, Darby. 2007. *How to See a Work of Art in Total Darkness*. Cambridge, MA: MIT Press.

Fanon, Frantz. 1970/1994. *Toward the African Revolution*. Translated by Haakon M. Chevalier New York: Grove Press.

Ferreira Da Silva, Denise. 2014. "Toward a Black Feminist Poethics: The Quest(ion) of Blackness toward the End of the World." *The Black Scholar* 44, no. 2: 81–97.

Forensic Architecture. 2011. "Left-to-Die Boat." Forensic Architecture. http://www.forensic-architecture.org/case/left-die-boat/.

Gaines, Charles. 2015. "Creative Time Summit: The Curriculum." Venice Biennale, August 11, http://livestream.com/creativetime/biennalearte/videos/95991585.

Glissant, Édouard. 1995/2006. *Poetics of Relation*. Translated by Betsy Wing. Ann Arbor: University of Michigan Press.

Glissant, Édouard, and Manthia Diawara. 2011. "One World in Relation: Édouard Glissant in Conversation with Manthia Diawara." *Nka, Journal of Contemporary African Art*, no. 28: 4–19.

Glover, Kaiama. 2011. "Comments on J. Michael Dash's 'Hemispheric Horizons.'" *Caribbean Commons: Caribbean Studies in the Northeast U.S.* January 20, https://caribbean.commons.gc.cuny.edu/2011/01/20/comments-on-j-michael-dashs-hemispheric-horizons/.

Goff, Phillip Attiba. 2014. "Black Boys Viewed as Older, Less Innocent Than Whites, Research Finds." American Psychological Association, March 6. http://www.apa.org/news/press/releases/2014/03/black-boys-older.aspx.

Gordon, Avery. 1998. *Ghostly Matters: Haunting and the Sociological Imagination*. Minneapolis: University of Minnesota Press.

Gordon, Lewis. 2007. "Through the Hellish Zone of Nonbeing: Thinking through Fanon, Disaster, and the Damned of the Earth." *Human Architecture: Journal of the Sociology of Self-Knowledge* 5, no. 3: 5–12.

Grim, Robert. 2012. "Robert Gibbs Says Anwar al-Awlaki's Son, Killed by Drone Strike, Needs 'Far More Responsible Father.'" *Huffington Post*, October 24, 2012, http://www.huffingtonpost.com/2012/10/24/robert-gibbs-anwar-al-awlaki_n_2012438.html.

Hanchard, Michael. 2008. "Black Memory versus State Memory: Notes to a Method." *Small Axe*, no. 26 (June): 45–62.

Harney, Stefano, and Fred Moten. 2013. *The Undercommons: Fugitive Planning and Black Study*. New York: Minor Compositions.

Harris, Claire. 1984. *Fables from the Women's Quarters*. Fredericton, NB: Goose Lane Editions.

Hartman, Saidiya. 2014. "Human Rights and the Humanities." YouTube video, 18: 09. March 20, https://www.youtube.com/watch?v=z8VsTaofizk.

———. 2008. "Venus in Two Acts." *Small Axe*, no. 26 (June): 1–14.

———. 2007. *Lose Your Mother: A Journey along the Atlantic Slave Route*. New York: Farrar, Straus, and Giroux.

———. 2002. "The Time of Slavery." *South Atlantic Quarterly* 101, no. 4: 757–777.

———. 1997. *Scenes of Subjection: Terror, Slavery, and Self-Making in Nineteenth-Century America*. New York: Oxford University Press.

Hartman, Saidiya V., and Frank B. Wilderson III. 2003. "The Position of the Unthought: An Interview with Saidiya V. Hartman conducted by Frank B. Wilderson, III." *Qui Parle* 13, no. 2: 183–201.

Hochschild, Adam. 2006. *Bury the Chains: Prophets and Rebels in the Fight to Free an Empire's Slaves*. New York: Houghton Mifflin Harcourt.

Holloway, Karla. 2002. *Passed On: African American Mourning Stories: A Memorial*. Durham, NC: Duke University Press.

Hurdle, John. 2013. "A Hospital Offers a Grisly Lesson on Gun Violence." *New York Times*, February 6, http://www.nytimes.com/2013/02/07/us/07philly.html?_r.

Hyde, Lewis. 2009. *The Gift: Creativity and the Artist in the Modern World*. New York: Knopf Doubleday.

Iton, Richard. 2013. "Still life." *Small Axe*, no. 17: 22–39.

———. 2010. *In Search of the Black Fantastic: Politics and Popular Culture in the Post–Civil Rights Era*. New York: Oxford University Press.

Jackson, Zakiyyah Iman. 2011. "Waking Nightmares." *GLQ: A Journal of Lesbian and Gay Studies* 17, nos. 2–3: 357–363.

Jacobs, Harriet A. 1861/1987. *Incidents in the Life of a Slave Girl: Written by Herself*. Edited by Jean Fagan Yellin. Cambridge, MA: Harvard University Press.

James, C. L. R. 1938/1989. *The Black Jacobins*. New York: Vintage.

James, Joy. 2014. "Afrarealism and the Black Matrix: Maroon Philosophy at Democracy's Border." *The Black Scholar* 44, no. 2: 124–131.

———. 2013. "Killing Mockingbirds: Cultural Memory and the Central Park Case." Paper presented at Tufts University, February 20.

James, Joy, and João Costa Vargas. 2012. "Refusing Blackness-as-Victimization: Trayvon Martin and the Black Cyborgs." In *Pursuing Trayvon: Historical Contexts and Contemporary Manifestations of Racial Dynamics*, edited by George Yancy and Janine Jones, 193–205. Latham, MD: Lexington Books.

Jefferson, Thomas. 1785/1998. *Notes on the State of Virginia*. New York: Penguin Classics.

Jeffries, Michael. 2013. "Obama's Chicago Speech Can't Address Gun Violence unless It Takes On Race." *The Atlantic*, February 15, http://www.theatlantic

.com/politics/archive/2013/02/obamas-chicago-speech-cant-address-gun
-violence-unless-it-takes-on-race/273200/.

Jordan, June. 2003. "The Difficult Miracle of Black Poetry in America or Something like a Sonnet for Phillis Wheatley." In *Some of Us Did Not Die: New and
Selected Essays.* New York: Basic Civitas Books.

Josephs, Kelly Baker. 2003. "Versions of X/Self: Kamau Brathwaite's Caribbean
Discourse." *Anthurium: A Caribbean Studies Journal* 1, no. 1.

Keene, John. 1995. *Annotations* (Vol. 809). New York: New Directions Publishing.

Kennedy, R. M. 2010. "National Dreams and Inconsolable Losses: The Burden of
Melancholia in Newfoundland Culture." In *Despite This Loss: Essays on Cul-
ture, Memory and Identity in Newfoundland and Labrador,* edited by Ursula A.
Kelly and Elizabeth Yeoman, 103–116. Newfoundland: Iser Books.

Kirchgaessner, Stephanie. 2015. "Five Men Charged with Murder of 200 Migrants
Drowned in the Med." August 7, http://www.theguardian.com/world/2015
/aug/07/italy-migrant-boat-capsize-five-men-accused-murder?CMP=share
_btn_tw.

Kotlowitz, Alex. 2013. "The Price of Public Violence." *New York Times,* February
24, http://www.nytimes.com/2013/02/24/opinion/sunday/the-price-of
-public-violence.html.

Lanzmann, Claude, dir. 1985. *Shoah.* New Yorker Films.

LeDuff, Charlie. 2010. "What Killed Aiyana Stanley-Jones?" *Mother Jones,* Novem-
ber/December, http://www.motherjones.com/politics/2010/11/aiyana
-stanley-jones-detroit.

Lewis, Andrew. 2007. "Martin Dockray and the Zong: A Tribute in the Form of a
Chronology." *Journal of Legal History* 28, no. 3: 357–370.

Llenín-Figueroa, Beatriz. 2014. "'I Believe in the Future of "Small Countries'":
Édouard Glissant's Archipelagic Scale in Dialogue with Other Caribbean
Writers." *Discourse* 36, no. 1: 87–111.

Macharia, Keguro. 2015. "Mbiti and Glissant." *New Inquiry,* March 9, http://
thenewinquiry.com/blogs/wiathi/mbiti-glissant/.

McKittrick, Katherine. 2014. "Mathematics Black Life." *Black Scholar* 44, no. 2:
16–28.

————. 2013. "Plantation Futures." *Small Axe,* no. 17: 1–15.

Mintz, Sidney. 1986. *Sweetness and Power: The Place of Sugar in Modern History.*
New York: Penguin.

Mirzoeff, Nicholas. 2011. *The Right to Look: A Counterhistory of Visuality.* Durham,
NC: Duke University Press.

Morgan, Jennifer. 2004. *Laboring Women: Reproduction and Gender in New World
Slavery.* Philadelphia: University of Pennsylvania Press.

Morrison, Toni. 1998. "Home." In *The House That Race Built: Original Essays by
Toni Morrison, Angela Y. Davis, Cornel West, and Others on Black Americans
and Politics in America Today,* edited by Wahneema Lubiano, 3–12. New York:
Vintage.

———. 1987. *Beloved*. New York: Plume Contemporary Fiction.

Moten, Fred. 2003. *In the Break: The Aesthetics of the Black Radical Tradition*. Minneapolis: University of Minnesota Press.

Neum, Efrat. 2014. "Afula Man Indicted for Trying to Kill Black Baby." *Ha'aretz*, January 16, http://www.haaretz.com/mobile/.premium-1.568956?v=41A3D 36E90F99AF017BE4CABEB21FEAC.

Nyong'o, Tavia. 2012. "Black Survival in the Uchromatic Dark." *Feminist Wire*, December 18, http://www.thefeministwire.com/2012/12/black-survival-in -the-uchromatic-dark/.

Nzengou-Tayo, Marie-Jose. 2006. "Kamau Braithwaite and the Haitian Boat People: *Dream Haiti* or the Nightmare of the Caribbean Intellectual." In *Caribbean Culture: Soundings on Kamau Braithwaite*, edited by Annie John, 176–187. Mona: University of West Indies Press.

Peart, Nicholas K. 2011. "Why Is the N.Y.P.D. After Me?" *New York Times*, Opinion section, December 17.

Philip, M. NourbeSe. 2008. *Zong!* Hartford, CT: Wesleyan University Press.

Pierre, Jemima. 2012. *The Predicament of Blackness: Postcolonial Ghana and the Politics of Race*. Chicago: University of Chicago Press.

Powell, Richard. 2008. *Cutting a Figure: Fashioning Black Portraiture*. Chicago: University of Chicago Press.

Raiford, Leigh, and Robin J. Hayes. 2014. "Remembering the Workers of the Domino Sugar Factory." *The Atlantic*, July, http://www.theatlantic.com /business/archive/2014/07/remembering-the-workers-of-the-domino -sugar-factory/373930/.

Rankine, Claudia. 2015. "The Condition of Black Life Is One of Mourning." *New York Times*, June 22, http://www.nytimes.com/2015/06/22/magazine/the -condition-of-black-life-is-one-of-mourning.html.

———. 2014. *Citizen: An American Lyric*. Minneapolis: Graywolf.

Rediker, Marcus. 2008. "History from below the Water Line: Sharks and the Atlantic Slave Trade." *Atlantic Studies: Global Currents* 5, no. 2: 285–297.

———. 2007. *The Slave Ship: A Human History*. New York: Penguin.

Reinhardt, Mark. 2010. *Who Speaks for Margaret Garner?* Minneapolis: University of Minnesota Press.

Roberts, Justin. 2013. *Slavery and the Enlightenment in the British Atlantic, 1750–1807*. Cambridge: Cambridge University Press.

Ruderman, Wendy. 2012. "For Women in Street Stops, Deeper Humiliation." *New York Times*, August 6, http://www.nytimes.com/2012/08/07/nyregion/for -women-in-street-stops-deeper-humiliation.html?_r=0.

Sambira, Jocelyne. 2015. "Historic 'Ark of Return' monument on slavery unveiled at the UN." Africa Renewal Online. March 25, http://www.un.org /africarenewal/web-features/historic-%E2%80%98ark-return%E2%80%99 -monument-slavery-unveiled-un.

Sargent, Antwaun. 2014. "Interview: Kara Walker Decodes Her New World

Sphinx at Domino Sugar Factory." *Complex*, May 13, http://www.complex
.com/style/2014/05/kara-walker-interview.
Saucier, P. Khalil, and Tryon Woods. 2014. "Ex Aqua: The Mediterranean Basin,
Africans on the Move, and the Politics of Policing." *Theoria* 61, no. 141
(December): 55–75.
Saunders, Patricia J. 2008a. "Defending the Dead, Confronting the Archive:
A Conversation with M. NourbeSe Philip." *Small Axe* 12, no. 2: 63–79.
———. 2008b. "Fugitive Dreams of Diaspora: Conversations with Saidiya Hart-
man." *Anthurium: A Caribbean Studies Journal* 6, no. 1: 7.
Schwartz, Marie Jenkins. 2010. *Birthing a Slave: Motherhood and Medicine in the
Antebellum South*. Cambridge, MA: Harvard University Press.
Sekula, Allan. 1995. *Fish Story*. Rotterdam: Richter Verlag.
Sekula, Allan, and Noël Burch. 2012. Allan Sekula and Noël Burch: The Forgotten
Space—panel discussion, April 24, http://www.tate.org.uk/context-comment
/video/allan-sekula-and-noel-burch-forgotten-space-panel-discussion.
———. 2011. "*The Forgotten Space*: Notes for a Film." *New Left Review* 69, 78–79.
———, dir. 2010. *The Forgotten Space—A Film Essay Seeking to Understand the
Contemporary Maritime World in Relation to the Symbolic Legacy of the Sea*.
Doc.Eye.
———. 2010. *The Forgotten Space*. http://www.theforgottenspace.net/static
/home.html.
Sexton, Jared. 2012. Ante-Anti-Blackness: Afterthoughts. *Lateral* 1, http://lateral
.culturalstudiesassociation.org/issue1/content/sexton.html.
———. 2006. Race, Nation, and Empire in a Blackened World. *Radical History
Review* 95: 250–261.
Sharpe, Christina. 2015. "Three Scenes." In *On Marronage: Ethical Confrontations
with Anti-Blackness*, edited by P. Khalil Saucier and Tryon P. Woods, 131–153.
Trenton, NJ: Africa World Press.
———. 2014. "Black Studies: In the Wake." *Black Scholar* 44, no. 2: 59–69.
———. 2012a. "Blackness, Sexuality, and Entertainment." *American Literary History* 24, no. 4: 827–841.
———. 2012b. "Response to Jared Sexton's 'Ante-Anti-Blackness: Afterthoughts.'" *Lateral* 1, http://lateral.culturalstudiesassociation.org/issue1
/content/sharpe.html.
———. 2010. *Monstrous Intimacies: Making Post-Slavery Subjects*. Durham, NC:
Duke University Press.
———. 1999. "The Work of Re-membering: Reading Gertrude Stein, Gayl Jones,
Julie Dash, Cherríe Moraga, and Bessie Head. Ph.D. dissertation, Cornell
University.
Silverstein, Jason. 2013. "I Don't Feel Your Pain." *Slate*, June 23, http://www.slate
.com/articles/health_and_science/science/2013/06/racial_empathy_gap
_people_don_t_perceive_pain_in_other_races.html.
Sissako, Abderrahmane, dir. 2014. *Timbuktu*. Cohen Media Group.

Smallwood, Stephanie. 2008. *Saltwater Slavery: A Middle Passage from Africa to American Diaspora*. Cambridge, MA: Harvard University Press.

Snorton, C. Riley. 2014. "What More Can I Say? (A Prose-Poem on Antiblackness)." *Feminist Wire*, September 3, http://www.thefeministwire.com/2014/09/can-say-prose-poem-antiblackness/.

————. 2014. *Nobody Is Supposed to Know: Black Sexuality on the Down Low*. Minneapolis: University of Minnesota Press.

Spillers, Hortense J. 2003a. "Interstices: A Small Drama of Words." In *Black, White and in Color: Essays on American Literature and Culture*, edited by Hortense Spillers, 152–175. Chicago: University of Chicago Press.

————. 2003b. "Mama's Baby, Papa's Maybe: An American Grammar Book." In *Black, White, and in Color: Essays on American Literature and Culture*, edited by Hortense Spillers, 203–229. Chicago: University of Chicago Press.

Stein, Rob. 2007. "At the End of Life, a Racial Divide." *Washington Post*, March 12, http://www.washingtonpost.com/wpdyn/content/article/2007/03/11/AR2007031101565.html.

Stillman, Sarah. 2013. "Lampedusa's Migrant Tragedy, and Ours." *New Yorker*, October 10, http://www.newyorker.com/news/daily-comment/lampedusas-migrant-tragedy-and-ours.

Stuckey, Sterling. 1992. "Slavery and the Circle of Culture." In *Society and Culture in the Slave South*, edited by J. William Harris, 100–127. New York: Routledge.

Taylor, Leon. 1994. "Man Killed by Cops after Pointing Gun." *Philadelphia Daily News*, June 22, http://articles.philly.com/1994-06-22/news/25835083_1_apartment-building-bomb-squad-officers.

Thompson, Robert Farris. 1984. *Flash of the Spirit: African and Afro-American Art and Philosophy*. New York: Vintage.

Tinsley, Omise'eke Natasha. 2010. *Thiefing Sugar: Eroticism between Women in Caribbean Literature*. Durham, NC: Duke University Press.

————. 2008. "Black Atlantic, Queer Atlantic: Queer Imaginings of the Middle Passage." *GLQ* 14, no. 2–3: 191–215.

Trethewey, Natasha. 2010. *Beyond Katrina: A Meditation on the Mississippi Gulf Coast*. Athens: University of Georgia Press.

Trouillot, Michel-Rolph. 1997. *Silencing the Past: Power and the Production of History*. Boston: Beacon.

Varga, Darrell. 2012. "Making Political Cinema—The Forgotten Space." In *A Film about the Sea: Notes on Allan Sekula and Noël Burch's* The Forgotten Space, 37–41. Halifax, NS: Halifax Centre for European Studies.

Vega, Tanzina. 2014. "Schools' Discipline for Girls Differs by Race and Hue." *New York Times*, December 11, http://www.nytimes.com/2014/12/11/us/school-discipline-to-girls-differs-between-and-within-races.html.

Vieux-Chauvet, Marie. 2009. *Love, Anger, Madness: A Haitian Triptych*. New York: Modern Library.

Walcott, Derek. 1987. "The Sea Is History." In *Collected Poems, 1948–1984*. New York: Farrar, Straus and Giroux.

Walcott, Rinaldo. Forthcoming. *The Long Emancipation*.

———. 2007. "Into the Ranks of Man: Vicious Modernism and the Politics of Reconciliation." In *Law and the Politics of Reconciliation*, 343–349. Hampshire, England: Ashgate Publishing Limited.

———. 2006. "Outside in Black Studies: Reading from a Queer Place in the Diaspora." In *Black Queer Studies: A Critical Anthology*, edited by E. Patrick Johnson and Mae G. Henderson, 90–105. Durham, NC: Duke University Press.

Walt, Vivienne. 2012. "Migrants Left to Die on the High Seas Continue to Haunt NATO." *Time*, April 17, http://content.time.com/time/world/article/0,8599,2112173,00.html.

Walvin, James. 2011. *The Zong: A Massacre, the Law and the End of Slavery*. New Haven, CT: Yale University Press.

Weheliye, Alexander G. 2014. *Habeas Viscus: Racializing Assemblages, Biopolitics, and Black Feminist Theories of the Human*. Durham, NC: Duke University Press.

———. 2014. "Introduction: black studies and black life." *The Black Scholar* 44.2: 5–10.

Wilderson, Frank. 2010. *Red, White, and Black: Cinema and the Structure of U.S. Antagonisms*. Durham, NC: Duke University Press.

Wright, Richard. 2007. *Black Boy: A Record of Childhood and Youth*. New York: Harper Perennial Modern Classics.

Wynter, Sylvia. 1994. "'No Humans Involved': An Open Letter to My Colleagues." *Forum N.H.I.: Knowledge for the 21st Century*, "Knowledge on Trial." 1, no. 1: 42–73.

———. 2006 "Proud/Flesh Interview with Sylvia Wynter." *ProudFlesh: A New Afrikan Journal of Culture, Politics and Consciousness* 4: 1–36.

Young, Harvey. 2010. *Embodying Black Experience: Stillness, Critical Memory, and the Black Body*. Ann Arbor: University of Michigan Press.

Young, Kevin. 2012. *The Grey Album: On the Blackness of Blackness*. Minneapolis: Graywolf.

———. 2011. *Ardency: A Chronicle of the Amistad Rebels*. New York: Knopf.

Youngquist, Paul. 2011. "The Mothership Connection." *Cultural Critique* 77 (Winter): 1–23.

INDEX

*

to health and education and, 5, 15, 33, 97; migration and, 15; mother/ing and, 15, 26–28, 43, 49, 57, 74, 77–81, 84, 87, 91, 140n6; non/being and, 5, 14–15, 20, 21, 74, 79, 86; non/status and, 15, 74, 79; ontological negation and, 14, 150n54; optics and, 21, 85–86, 99, 114–115, 124; pathologization of, 87; premature death and, 5, 15, 33, 97; signification and, 80–81; skewed life chances and, 5, 15, 33, 97; space and, 20; as specter, 82; terror and, 15, 20, 22, 73–74, 77, 79, 85, 116, 148n35; underdevelopment and, 34; violence and, 29, 79, 88–89; as weaponized, 16, 81

Black portraiture, 114–116

Black redaction, 113–118, 122–124, 126, 138n15; as counter to abandonment, 117; as counter to force of the state, 123. *See also* Wake work

Black resistance, 124

Black scholars, 12, 94

Black subjection, 5, 12

Black subjects, 14, 115

Black suffering, 16, 22, 53, 55, 93, 116, 127; human drama and, 53

Black un/children, 77; abandonment and, 89, 93; as "future criminals," 87, 147n34; resilience and, 92, 96; trauma and, 88–90, 92, 96–97

Black un/mothers, 77

Black Venus (Hartman), 51

Black women, 74, 77–78, 84, 87, 124, 147n30

Black Youth Project, 94, 149n46

Blanchot, Maurice, 5, 136n6, 137n6, 137n7, 152n22

Bland, Sandra, 87, 110

Blood-stained gate, 88

Bloomberg, Michael, 86, 92–93, 147n29, 149n43

Blubber (Gallagher), 140n2

Boroff, David, 149n47

Boyd, Rekia, 87, 110

Brand, Dionne, xi, 12, 14, 17, 25, 36, 47, 57–58, 68, 70, 83, 106–107, 109, 120, 130, 132–134, 136n6, 138n19, 139n25; on blackened knowledge, 13; on care, 131; on the door of no return, 32, 60, 131, 136n4, 141n10; interview with Maya Mavjee, 139n30, 149n45; on retina and attachments, 99, 136n4; and wake work, 18–19

Branding (marking), 48–49, 126, 148n41

Brathwaite, Kamau, 14, 34, 41, 57, 69, 77, 81, 108–109, 128, 145n15

Braun, Lundy, 111

Brawley, Otis, 138n16

Breathing Race into the Machine (Braun), 111

Breathing while Black, 84

Brenner, Yermi, 145n5

Britain, 71–72

Brookes plan diorama (ship illustration), 54, 148n41

Brooks, David: on Haiti, 33, 141n11, 154; on Tel Aviv, 33–34

Brown, Amanda Christy, 149n42

Brown, Kimberly Juanita, 151n13

Brown, Michael, 34, 82–83, 110, 123, 125

Brown, Vincent, 37

Brown v. Board of Education, 3

Browne, Simone, 148n41

Brutal Imagination (Eady), 82–83, 91

Buckley, Cara, 151n10

Burch, Noël, 25, 29, 31, 77, 140n4

Burnett, Charles, 124

Burruss, Logan, 147n32

Business Dictionary Online, 87

Calais, France, 71, 83, 144n2

Cameron, David, 71, 144n2

Campbell, Colin, 149n43

Canada, 52

sciousness of, 18–19, 141n10; the door of no return (Brand) and, 141n10; Haiti and, 128; survival in, 131

Diawara, Manthia, 69

Dickerson, Caitlin, 143n24

Diome, Fatou, 72, 130, 145n8, 152n23

Ditto ditto, 52, 56, 58–59, 73, 82, 94, 109, 142n15. *See also* Archives; *Zong!*

Domestic middle passage, 73–74, 79

Dominican Republic, 16, 53, 138–139n23

Domino Sugar Refining Plant, 98–99

Door, the (as optic), 4, 18, 23–25, 32, 55, 69–70, 79–81, 91, 99–100, 101, 105, 107, 121, 123, 131–132, 136n4, 138n19, 139n28, 141n10. *See also* Door of no return

Door of no return, 13, 17, 32, 99, 109, 131, 136n4; as alongside and counter to the archive, 131; as site of consciousness, 141n10. See also *Map to the Door of No Return* (Brand)

Dorner, Christopher, 149–150n49

Douglass, Frederick, 86, 155; on the blood-stained gate, 88; on everyday tyranny of slavery, 80

Drana, 43–45, 118–120, 151n15, 152n16. *See also* Daguerreotypes

Dreams Are Colder Than Death (film) (Jafa), 97

"Dream Haiti" (Brathwaite), 34, 41, 57, 81, 109, 128, 145n15

Dred Scott v. Sanford, 85–86

Dressner, Julie, 147n28

Dunn, Jordan, 87

Dutch Caribbean, 135n2

Dysgraphia, 21, 33, 96, 97, 115, 123, 131

Eady, Cornelius, 82

Ebola cartoon, 65

Edmonton Journal, 51

Edward Howard (ship), 104

Elgot, Jessica, 144n2

Elliott, Andrea, 90–93, 148n40

Ellison, Ralph, 60; the boomerang of history and, 60, 144n36. See also *Invisible Man*

Emancipation, 5, 14, 44, 105–106, 136n5

Emanuel African Methodist Episcopal Church, 16

End Credits (film), 114, 140n6

European Union (eu), 59, 72, 143n33, 145n8, 152n23

Exaqua (Philip), 38, 108

Facebook, 74, 87, 147n34

Fanon, Frantz, 20, 108, 111–112

Feeding the Ghosts (D'Augiar), 53

Ferguson, Missouri, 83, 97

Ferrell, Jonathan, 110

Fish Story (Sekula), 26

Forensic Architecture Project, 58–59

Forensic Oceanography, 59

The Forgotten Space — A Film Essay Seeking to Understand the Contemporary Maritime World in Relation to the Symbolic Legacy of the Sea (film) (Sekula and Burch), 25–26, 29, 77, 140n1

"Former mother," 27–28, 77, 87, 91, 140n6. See also Jackson, Aereile

For Those in Peril on the Sea (Locke installation), 65

Freedom, 42, 100; antiblackness and, 112; in *Beloved*, 103–104, Browne on, 149n41; Edwidge Danticat on, 105; in the Fugitive Slave Act, 104; Rinaldo Walcott on, 136n5; in the wake, 130

French Resistance, 69

Fugitive Slave Act, 104; "free air" and, 104, 112, "free state" and, 104

Furtive movements, 85–86

Gaines, Charles, 61–62, 67, 144n39

Gaine's Landing, Arkansas, 104–105

Gardulski, Anne, xi, 40–41, 142n16
Garner, Cilla, 104–105
Garner, Eric, 87, 110–111
Garner, Margaret, 104–105, 110, 150n3
Gates, Daryl, 109, 112
Gerima, Haile, 124
Germany, 4, 8, 34, 71, 144n4, 145n5, 145n6
Gibbs, Robert, 16, 156
Girl, 52–53, 76, 80–81, 91, 93, 95, 116, 121–123, 142n15, 145n12, 147n23; Phillis (Wheatley) as, 42–43, 45, 52–53, 89; with word "ship" on her forehead, 44–45, 48–53, 57, 92, 117–120, 132–133, 152n17. *See also* Girl holding ship; Hutchings, Mikia
Girl holding a ship (photograph), 46–48, 50, 57
Glissant, Édouard, 19, 69, 73
Glover, Kaiama, 47–50
Goff, Philip Attiba, 146n19
Grant, Oscar, 99, 100, 116
Greece, 4, 72
Gregson v. Gilbert, 35, 38, 45
Guadelope, Haiti, 60, 144n35. *See also* Haiti
Guardian, 92, 142n23, 143n32, 144n2, 147n24, 149n44
Guatemala, 50
Gun violence, 88, 90, 96–97, 148n35, 150n51

Hackman, Rose, 147n24
Haiti, 51, 60, 61, 83, 109, 153; arc of return and, 60; Beverly Bell on, 130; cholera and, 50; David Brooks on, 33; earthquake (2010) and, 44, 46, 79, 116, 117, 120, 130; ethnic cleansing in the Dominican Republic and, 16, 138–139n23; France and, 33, 60; refugees and, 46–48, 51–52, 57, 92, 142n20, 142n21, 143n26, 152n17; Zabou (Sissako) and, 128–130. *See*

also Girl; "Dream Haiti" (Brathwaite)
Haitian boat people, 46–48, 139n23, 142n20
Haitian refugees, 46–47, 57, 142n20
Hammon, Jupiter, 142n17
Harney, Stefano, 27, 138n18
Harris, Claire, 51–52
Hartman, Saidiya, 32, 57; Black Venus and, 51–52; on countering the violence of abstraction, 8; on the afterlives of chattel slavery, 5, 15, 33, 97; on the archives of slavery, 13, 18, 52, 132, 139n26; on the coffle, 73, 79; on the domestic middle passage, 73; on personhood and proper names, 115; on the position of the unthought, 30; on unusual violences enacted on Black people, 116; on "whites being the allies of blacks," 57
Hawthorne, Nathaniel, 80
Hayes, Robin J., 99, 159
Healing Hurt People: Center for Nonviolence and Social Justice, 89, 148n38
Hemings, Sally, 146n21
Hieroglyphics of the flesh (Spillers), 115
Hi Man (character), 132–133
Hiscock, John, 152n20
Henry Lewis (ship), 104
The Hold, 83, 89, 104, 143n23, 151; absence of personhood in, 94; accounts of in the contemporary, 71, 131; apparatus of, 100; beholding and, 99–101, 134; in *Beloved*, 48; birth canal and, 74; in Black everydays, 32, 113; Black suffering in, 127; Calais and, 71; departures and arrivals in, 69; as destination, 124; door to, 55; family in the wake of, 91; Ferguson, Missouri, and, 83; former mother and, 140n6; Frank Wilderson on,

14, 138n20; Fugitive Slave Act and, 104; horrors of the holding in, 55; Hortense Spillers on, 73; inhabitation of, 69; iron bars of ballast of, 36; Kärcher and, 71; keepers of, 70; as lager, 108; language of violence in, 69, 100, 71; as location of Black being, 16, 124; logics of, 91, 97, 100; long wake of, 70; marital metaphors and, 91, 144n3; migrants and, 108; migrant ship and, 27; mothering and, 78; multiplication of, 73; Oscar Grant in, 100; policing and, 34, 100; as prison, 27, 75; repetition of in the classroom and hospital, 90; residence time of, 70; semiotics of the slave ship and, 21; slave ship and, 27, 75; suffocation and, 55, 111, 151n11; surveillance and, 91; survival of on the slave ship, 18–19, 111–112; violences of, 14, 37, 47, 80, 100, 130; William and, 92; as womb, 27. *See also* The Stop

Hollande, Jacques, 60, 144n35
Holloway, Jonathan, 87
Holocaust, 11, 34, 69, 136n6, 144n4
"Home" (Morrison), 117
Huggler, Justin, 144n4
Humanitarian patrols, 59, 143n33
Human trafficking, 59, 61, 70–71, 139n23
Hume, Tim, 146n17
Hurdle, John, 88–89, 93, 148n35, 157
Hurricane Katrina, 33, 44, 72, 79, 116
Hurricane Sandy, 34, 79, 146n17
Hutchings, Mikia, 81–82, 120, 121–123
Hyde, Lewis, 99, 157

Imaging the Black Body and Re-Staging Histories (2015 conference), 114
Imaging blackness, 114–116. *See also* Daguerreotypes; Imagining blackness

Imagining blackness, 20–22, 89, 113–117, 124, 128
Imperialism, 3, 15, 57, 61, 113
Indigo, 126–130
Insurance trade, 29–30, 35–38, 45, 110, 142n15. *See also* Slavery
International Day of Remembrance of the Victims of the Transatlantic Slave Trade, 61. See also *The Ark of Return*
Intramural, the (Spillers), 20, 101, 114
Inventory (Brand), 58
"Invisible Child" (Elliot), 90–93, 143n30, 149n42
Invisible Man (Ellison), 144n36

Jack, 43–44, 120, 151n15. *See also* Daguerreotypes; Zealy, Joseph T.
Jackson, Aereile, 27–32, 77, 91, 140n6. *See also* "Former mother"
Jafa, Arthur, 97, 124
James, C. L. R., 98–99
James, Joy, 7, 78, 97, 100
Jefferson, Thomas, 53, 78, 111, 146n21
Jeffries, Michael, 150n51
Jim Crow, 44, 106
Johnson, Albert, 68–69, 99, 144n1
Jones, Monica, 86
Jordan, June, 41, 43, 49, 52

Kennedy, R. M., 139n27
King, Rodney, 110, 116
Kleeman, Sophie, 143n24
Kotlowitz, Alex, 89–90, 97
Krase, Kathryn, 143n24
Kurtzman, Lori, 147n28

Lager, 71, 83, 108, 132
Lampédouzeans (Hazoumè), 66
Lampedusa (Italy), 4, 29, 53, 58, 70, 83, 108, 143n29
Lanzmann, Claude (Shoah), 11
LeDuff, Charlie, 146n22

Sissako, Abderrahmane, 27, 127–128, 152n21
Sixo (character), 128
Slaveholding class, 98
Slavery, 8, 11–16, 18, 20, 26, 29, 32–35, 38, 41, 43–44, 49, 55, 58, 60, 63, 69, 75, 78, 80, 97, 99, 100, 104, 112–113, 126–127, 130, 132, 137n6, 141n14, 142n18, 144n35, 146n21; administrative logics of, 106, 111, 117; afterlives of, 77; Douglass's blood-stained gate of, 88; monuments and memorials of, 61–62, 144n38; as singularity, 106, 109, 124, 134, 141n12; ungendering of slaves (Spillers), 50, 73–74, 79, 105. *See also* Transatlantic slavery
Slave ship. *See* The Ship
Slave Ship: Slavers Throwing Overboard Dead and Dying— Typhon Coming On (Turner), 36
Smallwood, Stephanie, 46
Smith, Cardinale, 138n16
Smith, Susan, 82–83
Smith, Yvette, 87
Snorton, C. Riley, 140n9
Somalia, 29
The Sound I Saw (DeCarava), 132
Spillers, Hortense, 52, 73, 75; archives and, 52; on Black life, 77; on the Black woman, 78; on the hieroglyphics of the flesh, 115; "Interstices: A Small Drama of Words" and, 49, 50, 52, 74, 76, 77, 79, 101, 115; on the intramural, 101; on the invasion of the state, 78; "Mama's Baby, Papa's Maybe: An American Grammar Book" and, 78–79; on ungendering, 50, 73–74, 79
Spirometer, 111–112, 154. *See also* Aspiration; Braun, Lundy; Shaban, Hamza
S/place, 30, 89
Srebnik, Simon, 11–12
Stanley-Jones, Aiyana, 81, 110, 146

State of the Union Address, 95–96, 149n49, 150n50
Stein, Rob, 10, 138n16
Still: in *Beloved*, 118,120, in *Verso* 55, 120
The Stop (police), 51, 83–87, 110; carding and, 83, 132; Eric Garner and, 110; "furtive movements" and, 85–86; gender and, 51, 84–85; rubric of, 85; sexuality and desire and, 87; stop-and-frisk, 15, 78, 83–87, 132, 147n26, 147n28, 147n29
A Subtlety (Walker), 98
Sugar, 99
Syphilis experiments, 50

Tapper, Jake, 146n18
Taylor, Kate, 147n29
Taylor, Matthew, 144n2
Telegraph, 144n2, 144n4, 152n20
Temple University Hospital, 88–89, 93, 148n36, 148n37. *See also* Cradle2Grave
Tepfer, Daniel, 145n14
Terror, 5, 15, 20, 22, 73–74, 77, 79, 85, 90, 116, 148n35
Thirsty (Brand), 68–70
Timbuktu (film), 127–130, 152n21; as wake work, 130
Time, 17, 27, 44, 74, 100, 118, 127, 128, 130; Abderrahmane Sissako on, 27; as anagrammatical, 76; Black girls and, 51–52; daguerreotype and, 120; disaster and, 5, 15; "Dream Haiti" (Brathwaite) and, 57, 128; monumental time, 62; ruptures in, 12; singularity and, 106; ship time, 62; slavery and, 106, 112, 126; of The Wake, 16, 19, 22, 41, 112; The Weather and, 106; Zabou (Sissako) and, 128. *See also* Residence time
Tinsley, Omise'eke, 19, 30
Tornado Alley, 34
Toronto, Canada, 68, 83

9, 62; position of the no-citizen in, 22; possibility in, 105; power of, 10; as a problem of and for thought, 5; residence time of, 19, 22, 41, 120, 128; "Ruttier for the Marooned in the Diaspora" (Brand) and, 107, 131, 133; of slavery, 8, 15, 18, 20, 50, 112, 116, 130, 132; social media and, 74; teaching in, 10; theory and praxis of, 19, 22; *Timbuktu* (film) and, 127; transverse waves of, 57; traumas left in, 97; un/survival and, 14, 37, 73, 93, 120, 131; water patterns of the ship and, 24, 38–40, 57, 111; weather of, 105, 111; willful disasters of, 94, 105; work in, 18, 19; of the *Zorgue* (slave ship), 120. *See also* Care; Dysgraphia; The Hold; Orthography of the wake; The Ship; Wake work; The Weather

Wake work, 13–14, 17–22, 33, 53, 59, 109, 113, 130; as aspiration, 109; as praxis of imagining, 18, 113. *See also* Wake theory

Wake theory, 19–20, 22

Walcott, Derek, 57

Walcott, Rinaldo, 74, 136

Walker, Kara, 97–99, 140n2

Walvin, James, 36, 141n13, 141n13, 141n15

Washington Post, 145n13, 147n25

Wayne, Pennsylvania, 3, 9, 136

The Weather, 75, 77, 81, 102, 134, 138n15, 140n6, 141n12, 143n23; aspiration and, 113; as atmospheric condition of time and place, 106, 132; *Beloved* and, 104–105; Black death and, 124; in Black everydays, 32; Black suffering and, 127; as contemporary conditions of Black life and death, 132; ecologies of, 106, 112; Lizzie Dear-

den on, 108; as location of Black being, 16, 106; lungs and, 112; as machine, 111; migrant boats and, 107; media and, 104; Morrison on, 104; orthography of, 20; plantation management and monitoring of, 112; as possibility, 105, 134; "Ruttier for the Marooned in the Diaspora" (Brand) and, 107; and slavery, 106; and slave ships, 102–103, 106, 112; as the totality of (anti)black environments and climate, 21, 104–107, 111; un/survival of, 18, 21, 120, 124, 127, 131, 134; of the wake, 111. *See also* The Hold; The Ship; The Wake

Weekley, Joseph, 81

Weisenburger, Steven, 150n3

Wheatley, Phillis, 41–43, 45, 49, 52–53, 78, 89, 142n17. *See also* Girl

Wilderson, Frank, 11, 14, 28–30, 57, 138n20, 141n10

William, 92–93, 149n44

Williams, Caleb, 6–8, 138n15

Wilson, Darren, 82–83, 145n13, 147n25

Wintour, Patrick, 144n2

Womb to tomb, 87

Woods, Tryon P., 55, 143n31

Wright, Richard, 74–75, 145n9

Wynter, Sylvia, 13, 92

Zabou, 127–130, 152n21. *See also* *Timbuktu*

Zealy, Joseph T., 120, 151n15

Zimmerman, George, 111, 151n10

Zong! (Philip), 19, 33, 38–40, 53, 69, 94, 108–109, 127

Zong (slave ship), 34–39, 45, 50, 52–53, 55, 69, 73, 109, 127, 141–142n15

Zorgue (slave ship), 34–35, 45, 50, 120

CPSIA information can be obtained
at www.ICGtesting.com
Printed in the USA
LVHW041924240223
740361LV00004B/488